PERCUSSION EDITION

BOOK ONE

Band Expressions™

Band Expressions Author Team

Percussion Author: James Campbell

Co-Lead Author: Robert W. Smith

Co-Lead Author: Susan L. Smith

Michael Story   Garland E. Markham   Richard C. Crain

Contributor: Linda J. Gammon

Editor: Thom Proctor

Consulting Editor: Patrick Roszell

Art Credits: page 5, *Butterfly II* by Paul Giovanopoulos, ©1995 Paul Giovanopoulos c/o Theispot Showcase;
page 34, *Scenes of Daily Life in Korea* by Kim Junkeun, ©Christies Images Ltd. 1995;
page 38, *Celebration 1975* by Charles Searles, ©Smithsonian American Art Musuem, Washington D.C./Art Resource, NY.

Expressions Music Curriculum™, Music Expressions™, Band Expressions™, Jazz Expressions™,
Orchestra Expressions™, and Guitar Expressions™
are trademarks of Alfred Publishing Co., Inc. All Rights Reserved.

3 4 5 6 7 8 9 10   10 09 08 07 06
© 2003 ALFRED PUBLISHING CO., INC.
All Rights Reserved

The Art of Playing Snare Drum

Instrument and Parts

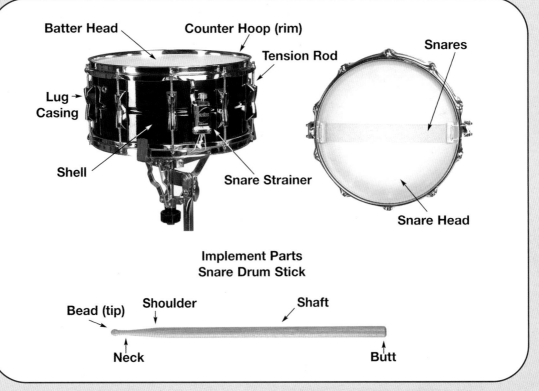

Batter Head — Counter Hoop (rim) — Tension Rod — Snares

Lug Casing

Shell — Snare Strainer

Snare Head

Implement Parts
Snare Drum Stick

Bead (tip) — Shoulder — Shaft

Neck — Butt

Assembly Procedure

1. The snare drum should be flat and parallel to the floor with the snare strainer placed directly in front of the player.

2. Adjust the stand to bring the top head to approximately waist level or slightly below.

3. It may be helpful to mark the stand height with a felt marker to ensure a consistent setup every time the instrument is assembled. This can be checked from time to time as you grow.

Care and Maintenance

- Use a cloth to keep the entire drum clean and free of fingerprints, dust, and dirt.

- Keep all objects off of the drum head; it's not a table.

- The average life of a drum head is less than one year. Replace worn or damaged heads immediately.

- A small dab of lithium grease or lubrication should be applied to the tension rods when the heads are replaced.

Disassembly Procedure

1. Store the drum and stand in its case with the snares engaged when not in use.

2. Cases are for your instrument only, not for sticks, music, folders, or books.

3. Store the sticks in a stick bag with all of your mallets and accessories.

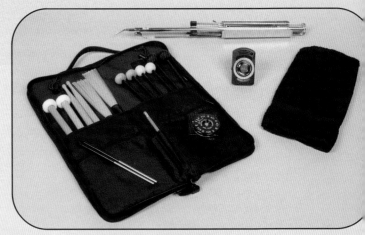

Supplies

- Snare Drum Sticks, concert model, pair
- General timpani mallets, pair
- Plastic bell mallets, pair
- Triangle beaters, pair
- Yarn mallets, pair
- Hard rubber mallets, pair
- Brushes, pair

- Pitch pipe (timpani tu
- Stick towel (black hand towel)
- Stick/Mallet Bag
- Drum key
- Metronome
- Pencil
- Wire Music Stand

The Art of Playing Snare Drum

Rest Position

Ready Position

Play Position

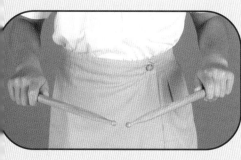

Grip

The stick should be placed diagonally across the palm of the hand. Grip the stick between the fleshy part of your thumb and the first joint of your index finger, approximately 1/3 the way up from the butt end of the stick to create the pivot point.

Gently close the remaining fingers around the stick for support.

Palms should face the floor with the thumbs on the side and all knuckles visible.

Tuning

The batter head should be tensioned until a natural rebound feels comfortable with the stick. The snare head should be tuned slightly higher than the batter head.

Tap softly on the batter head as you turn the control knob on the snare strainer to adjust the snare tension. The desired sound should be crisp and resonant.

- The shoulders are relaxed, the upper arms hang naturally, and the elbows are even with the sides and comfortably close to your body.

- Keep the forearms slightly below parallel to the floor.

- Stand away from the drum at a distance that puts the tips of the sticks slightly past the center of the head where they form an angle of approximately 75 degrees.

- The tips should be at rest in the ready position 1"-2" above the head.

- The proper playing area is slightly off center with the tips close together.

- From the ready position, use the wrist to raise the tip of the stick to the playing position about 12" above the drum head. Move the stick as far back as wrist movement will allow without moving the forearm.

- Move to the playing position when everyone takes a breath with the conductor's motion on the beat before you play. Develop a full stroke with just the motion of the wrist.

- Throw the stick toward the surface and allow the stick to immediately rebound back to the playing position.

- For successive strokes, the wrist should follow the natural rebound of the stick back to the playing position. The sticks may return to the ready position when there is a rest in the music.

- The full stroke will be affected by volume (dynamics) and speed (tempo).

- The softer that one plays, the closer to the surface one must start.

- Slower strokes naturally tend to require a greater range of motion than faster strokes

The Art of Playing Bass Drum

Instrument and Parts

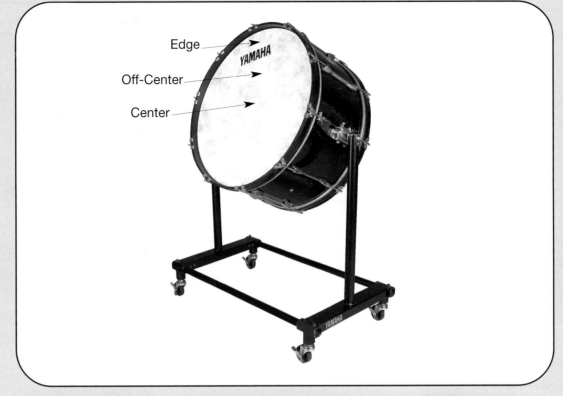

Edge
Off-Center
Center
YAMAHA

Setup Procedure

1. Drum should be tilted to reflect sound toward the conductor and the audience.

2. Set the music stand so that you can see the bass drum head, the music and the conductor.

3. Match the size of your bass drum beater to the size of your drum. A good general beater has a soft felt covering over a hard core.

Playing Areas

1. Off center - Strike the head here to produce the low resonant tone used for most playing situations.

2. At center - Strike the head here for the driest sound, when clarity is needed for quick repeated passages, o to create a cannon-shot effect.

3. Edge - Play with two mallets near the edge when producing rolls.

Care and Maintenance

- Use a cloth to keep the entire drum clean and free of fingerprints, dust, and dirt.

- Keep all objects off of the drum head; it's not a table.

Tuning

- The playing side is tuned low to achieve a deep, resonant tone. Tune the resonating head slightly higher than the playing side.

The Art of Playing Bass Drum

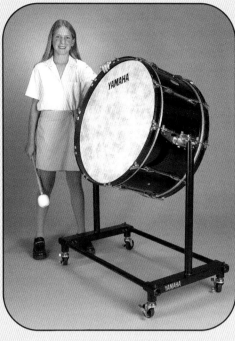

Rest Position

- The grip for the bass drum mallet is the same as that for the snare drum.

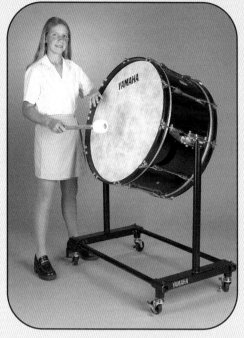

Ready Position

- Hold the stick with the right hand and use the left hand to muffle the head.

Play Position

- Throw the mallet directly toward the surface and allow it to rebound back to the starting position in one smooth motion. A full stroke uses the full motion of the wrist with a relaxed arm movement that adds weight to the stroke to produce a loud volume.

- Softer volumes are produced with just the motion of the wrist.

- Always allow the beater to naturally rebound off the head.

- Rolls are always single alternating strokes.

Dampen Position

- The bass drummer will often dampen to match their articulation and resonance to that of the low brass section. Lightly dampen with the fingers of the free hand during the stroke to control the articulation while playing. Dampen with the fingers and hand after the stroke is made to control the amount of sustain.

- Experiment with hand placement and pressure to determine the best sound for the bass drum in each musical situation.

- Use your stick towel to drape over the edge of the head for increased muffling.

UNIT 1 WILL BE PRESENTED BY YOUR TEACHER

The Art of Playing Timpani

Instrument and Parts

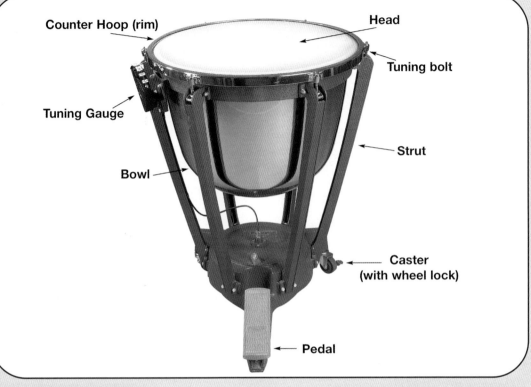

Counter Hoop (rim)
Head
Tuning bolt
Tuning Gauge
Strut
Bowl
Caster (with wheel lock)
Pedal

Assembly Procedure

1. The pedals should face the player, pointed slightly in toward the player.

2. Stand behind the timpani with feet comfortably spread apart. Sitting on a stool will help the taller player to better position the arms properly and to work the pedals more efficiently.

Disassembly Procedure

1. Keep the timpani covered when not in use.

2. Keep the timpani mallets in a storage bag when not in use. Avoid touching the felt with your hands.

Timpani Ranges

- Set each timpano into proper range by tuning the head to its fundamental note when the pedal is at its lowest position.

- 32" – D, 29" – F, 26" – B♭, 23" - d

Care and Maintenance

- Use a cloth to keep the entire timpano clean and free of fingerprints, dust, and dirt.

- Keep all objects off of the drum head; it's not a table.

- When you move the timpani, handle them only by the struts to avoid causing stress to the head.

- The average life of a timpani head is one to three years. Replace worn or damaged heads immdeiately.

Tuning

- Sound and listen to the tuning note at least five seconds (pitch pipe).

- Sing or hum to match the pitch.

- Turn your head to keep the ear close to the timpani head.

- Think the pitch; don't hum while you pedal the drum.

- With the pedal in its lowest position, tap softly, once with the mallet and pedal-up (glissando) until you reach the desired pitch.

- Check the tuning with another soft mallet tap and adjust if necessary.

The Art of Playing Timpani

Rest Position

Ready Position

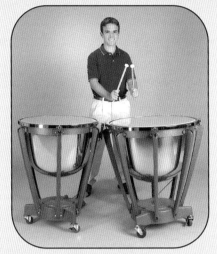

Play Position

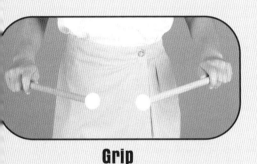

Grip

- The mallet should be placed diagonally across the palm of the hand. Grip the mallet between the fleshy part of your thumb and the first joint of your index finger near the end of the shaft. Approximately 1" of the mallet end should extend past the heel of your hand, just outside of the wrist.

- Gently close the remaining fingers around the stick for support. These fingers are always in contact with the mallet and move with the shaft.

- Palms should face the floor with the thumbs on the side and all knuckles visible.

- The shoulders are relaxed, the upper arms hang naturally, and the elbows are even with the sides and comfortably close to the body.

- Keep the forearms slightly below parallel to the floor.

- Stand away from the pair of timpani at a distance that puts the heads of the mallets at least 4"-5" from the edge of the bowl in a playing area that is directly over the pedal.

- The mallet heads should be at rest in the ready position 1" above and parallel to the head.

- The mallets should form a "V" with the mallet heads 6" apart when both mallets play the same timpano.

Dampen Position

- Dampen with the last three fingers of either hand after the stroke is made to control the amount of sustain.

- Develop a full legato stroke with a combination of arm, wrist, and finger motion. Move to the playing position when everyone takes a breath or with the conductor's motion on the beat before you play.

- From the ready position, use the forearm and wrist to raise the mallet head to the playing position about 18" above the drum head. The hand follows the mallet upward and remains in-line and below the mallet.

- Throw the mallet toward the surface and allow it to rebound naturally back to the playing position in one smooth continuous motion. The best tone is achieved when the mallet naturally rebounds off the head.

- The fingers should extend with the rebound of the mallet after it makes contact with the head. The fingers will move the stick back into the palm as the stick returns to the playing position.

- For successive strokes, the arm and wrist should follow the natural rebound of the mallet back to the playing position. The mallets may return to the ready position when there is a rest in the music.

- Turn from the waist to play both drums in the correct playing area.

- The full legato stroke will be affected by volume (dynamics) and speed (tempo).

  - The softer that one plays, the closer to the surface one must start.

  - Slower strokes naturally tend to require a greater range of motion than faster strokes.

The Art of Playing Bongos

Setup Procedure

1. Although bongos are traditionally played with the hands in a seated position, they can also be attached to a stand and played with snare drum sticks.

2. The drums should be flat and parallel to the floor. Adjust the stand to bring the top head to approximately waist level or slightly below.

3. The high drum may be placed on either the player's right or left to best accommodate the music

 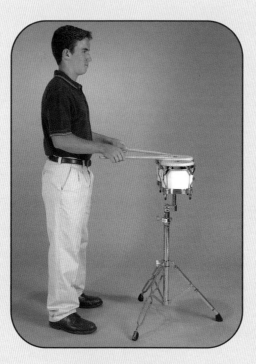 

| **Rest Position** | **Ready Position** | **Play Position** |

- The basic matched grip is the same as that for snare drum.

- Use the same ready position as that for snare drum.

- Use the same full stroke as that for snare drum.

Care and Maintenance

- Use a cloth to keep the entire drum clean and free of fingerprints, dust, and dirt.

- Keep all objects off of the drum head; it's not a table.

- The average life of a drum head is one year. Replace worn or damaged heads immediately.

- A small dab of lithium grease or lubrication should be applied to the tension rods when the heads are replaced.

Tuning

- The bongo heads should be tensioned until a natural rebound feels comfortable with the stick.

- The drums should be tuned about a fourth apart in pitch.

- The proper playing area is slightly off center on each drum.

UNIT 2

The Art of Playing Suspended Cymbal

Instrument and Parts

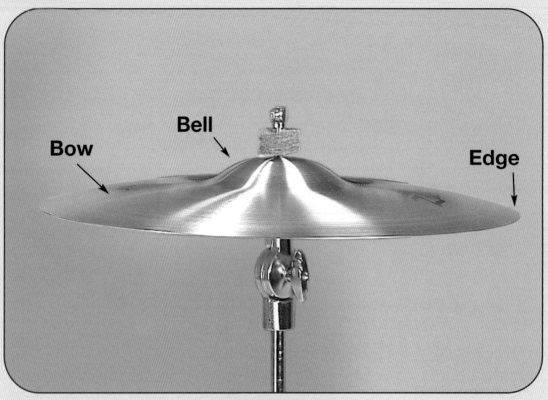

Bow   Bell   Edge

Setup Procedure

- The cymbal should be flat and parallel to the floor. Adjust the stand to bring the cymbal plate to approximately waist level.

Care and Maintenance

- Use a dry cloth or a mild solution of warm water and dish soap to keep the cymbal clean and free of fingerprints and stick marks.

- Use a professional cymbal cleaner for deep cleaning.

- Replace worn or missing washers and sleeves as needed. The cymbal stand should be free of rattles and unwanted noises.

Rest Position

- For both snare drum sticks and yarn mallets, the basic matched grip is the same as that for snare drum.

The Art of Playing Suspended Cymbal

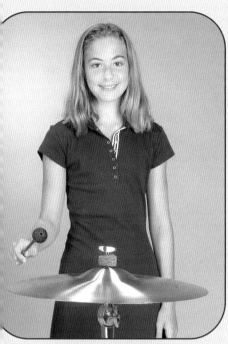

Ready Position

- Use a similar, but lower stroke than that for snare drum. Strike the surface of the cymbal between the bell and the edge to produce a shimmering tone.

Play Position

- Play with the shoulder of the stick on the edge for a sustained crash sound.

- Play the cymbal with snare drum sticks about halfway from the edge to the dome for an articulate "ride" effect.

Dampen Position

- Dampen with either hand after the stroke is made to control the amount of sustain.

Play Position

Strike directly on the bell for a special effect.

Ready Position

- Play with two mallets near the edge and on opposite sides when producing rolls.

- Use single alternating strokes for rolls.

The Art of Playing Keyboard Percussion

Instrument and Parts

Orchestra Bells/Glockenspiel

The narrow metal tone bars are arranged in two rows similar to the piano keyboard. Play with plastic or hard rubber mallets. The bells sound two octaves higher than written.

Xylophone

The narrow, thick wood or synthetic tone bars are arranged in two rows similar to the piano keyboard. Play with hard rubber mallets. The xylophone sounds one octave higher than written.

Assembly Procedure

1. All keyboard instruments should be flat and parallel to the floor.

2. Many keyboard have height-adjustable frames or stands. The height should be adjusted to waist level or slightly below.

Marimba

The wide, thin wood or synthetic tone bars are arranged in two rows similar to the piano keyboard. Play with yarn or hard rubber mallets. The marimba sounds as written.

Vibraphone/Vibes

The wide, thin metal tone bars are arranged in two rows similar to the piano keyboard. Play with yarn mallets. A dampening bar controls sustain with the use of a foot pedal. The vibraphone sounds as written.

Disassembly Procedure

1. Keep the keyboard percussion instruments covered when not in use.

2. Store your mallets in a bag with all of your sticks and accessories.

Care and Maintenance

- Use a cloth to keep the entire instrument clean and free of fingerprints, dust, and dirt.
- Avoid using furniture polish on wood tone bars as it leaves a residue.
- Keep all objects off of the bars; it's not a table.

The Art of Playing Keyboard Percussion

Rest Position

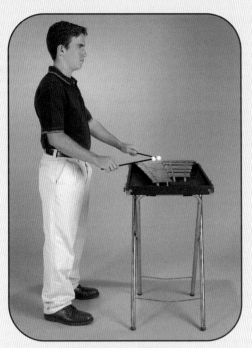

Ready Position

Play Position

Grip

The mallet should be placed diagonally across the palm of the hand. Grip the mallet between the fleshy part of your thumb and the first joint of your index finger so that approximately 1"-2" of the mallet end extends past the heel of your hand, just outside of the wrist.

Gently close the remaining fingers around the stick for support. These fingers are always in contact with the mallet and move with the shaft.

Palms should face the floor with the thumbs on the side and all knuckles visible.

- The shoulders are relaxed, the upper arms hang naturally, and the elbows are even with the sides and comfortably close to your body.

- Keep the forearms slightly below parallel to the floor.

- Stand away from the keyboard at a distance that puts the heads of the mallets over the center of the lower row of tone bars.

- The mallet heads should be at rest in the ready position 1" above the tone bars.

- The mallets should form a "V" with the angle of the mallet shafts at approximately 90 degrees.

- Keyboard percussion requires a lower full stroke than the snare drum and timpani because of the horizontal movement required when moving between tone bars.

- Using primarily a wrist motion, develop a lower full stroke with just the motion of the wrist. Move to the playing position when everyone takes a breath or with the conductor's motion on the beat before you play.

- From the ready position, use the wrist to raise the ball of the mallet to the playing position about 4"-6" above the tone bars. Move the mallets without moving the forearm.

- Throw the mallet, from the wrist, toward the tone bar and quickly lift it back to the playing position in one smooth continuous motion. Since the tone bar lacks the natural elasticity of a drumhead, you must supply some lift to bring the mallet back to the playing position. The best tone is achieved when the mallet is immediately lifted off the tone bar

- The proper playing area is the center of the tone bar. When two mallets play the same bar they should "split" the center with the left mallet closer to the music.

- Keep the mallets and wrist low to the keyboard while playing. Move the forearms, from the shoulder, in a flat horizontal motion to move the distance between tone bars. Avoid raising the forearms or turning the wrist to reach tone bars.

- The mallets may return to the ready position when there is a rest in the music.

- Keep your eyes on the music and use peripheral vision to locate the tone bars.

Creative Tools of Music (Units 2 and 3)

Articulation—a slight interruption of the air stream with the tongue

 Bar Line—a vertical line placed on a staff to divide music into measures

' Breath Mark—a recommended place to breathe

Clef—placed at the beginning of the staff to identify the note names

Embouchure—the natural formation of the facial and lip muscles on the mouthpiece or reed

Fermata—hold the note or rest longer than note value

Final Bar Line—indicates the end of a piece of music

♭ Flat—lowers the pitch of a note one half step

Grand Staff—treble and bass clef staves joined together

Interval—the distance between two pitches

Ledger Lines—short lines placed above or below the staff

Measure—the space between two bar lines to form a grouping of beats

Musical Alphabet—the letter names of the no used in music

Rhythm—the organization of sound and silen in time

♯ Sharp—raises the pitch of a note one half step

Staff—5 lines and 4 spaces on which notes are placed

Time Signature—a symbol placed at the beginning of the staff indicating the number of beats per measure and what kind of note g one beat

4/4 4 beats per measure
quarter note receives one beat

Musical Alphabet Games

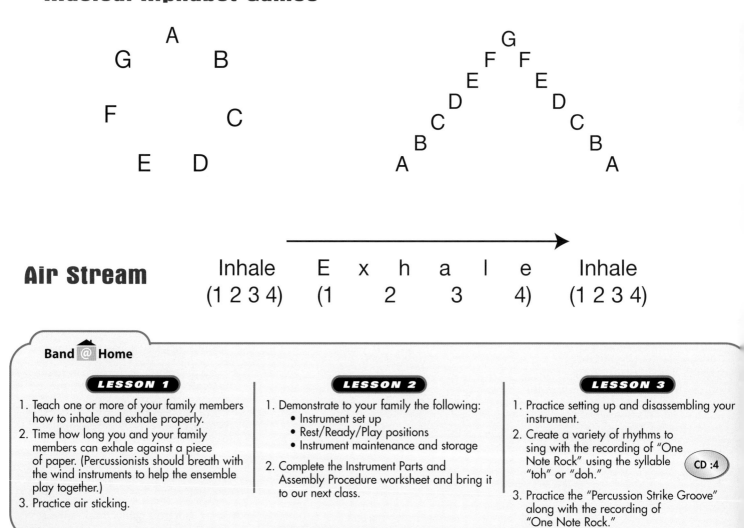

Air Stream   Inhale   E x h a l e   Inhale
(1 2 3 4)   (1   2   3   4)   (1 2 3 4)

Band @ Home

LESSON 1

1. Teach one or more of your family members how to inhale and exhale properly.
2. Time how long you and your family members can exhale against a piece of paper. (Percussionists should breath with the wind instruments to help the ensemble play together.)
3. Practice air sticking.

LESSON 2

1. Demonstrate to your family the following:
   • Instrument set up
   • Rest/Ready/Play positions
   • Instrument maintenance and storage
2. Complete the Instrument Parts and Assembly Procedure worksheet and bring it to our next class.

LESSON 3

1. Practice setting up and disassembling your instrument.
2. Create a variety of rhythms to sing with the recording of "One Note Rock" using the syllable "toh" or "doh."   **CD :4**
3. Practice the "Percussion Strike Groove" along with the recording of "One Note Rock."

Note Instructions for non-keyboard percussion instruments

Butterfly II, by Paul Giovanopoulos

©1995 Paul Giovanopoulos c/o Theispot Showcase

$\frac{4}{4}$ Conducting Pattern

1 First Sounds
* Strike once on any percussion instrument and allow the sound to decay naturally.

Set Ready Breathe
1   2   (3 4)

F ——————————————————→

2 Mouthpiece Rock

CD :5

——— Play two times ———

Set Ready Breathe
1   2   (3 4)

F →   R e s t   F →   R e s t

R R R R   L L L L
1 2 3 4 1 2 (3 4) 1 2 3 4 1 2 (3 4)

3 First Note
* Play Stroke Dexterity Exercises as assigned by your teacher.

CD :6

Set Ready Breathe
1   2   (3 4)

F ——————————————————→

4 One Note Shout
Keyboard Percussion Only

CD :7

——— Play two times ———

Set Ready Breathe
1   2   (3 4)

F ———→   R e s t   F ———→   R e s t

1 2 3 4   1 2 (3 4)   1 2 3 4   1 2 (3 4)

5 One Note Reggae
* Play Percussion Strike Groove as assigned by your teacher.

CD :8

Set Ready Breathe
1   2   (3 4)

F ——————→ | F →| F →| F | F | F | F | Rest ——————→   go to next line

1   2   3   4   1   2   3   4   1   2   3   4   1   2   3   4

F ——————→ | F | F | F | F | F →| F →| F →| Rest →

1   2   3   4   1   2   3   4   1   2   3   4   1   2   3   4

Band @ Home

LESSON 1

1. Practice "Mouthpiece Rock" with the recorded accompaniment.

2. Demonstrate for your family how to produce the first sounds on your instrument.

3. Perform "Mouthpiece Rock" with the accompaniment track for your family.

4. Practice Stroke Dexterity Exercise #1 in front of a mirror to observe your sticking motion. Stroke Dexterity Exercises are found in the back of the book.

LESSON 2

1. Perform "One Note Shout" with the accompaniment track for your family and/or friends.

2. Practice Stroke Dexterity Exercises #1–4.

LESSON 3

1. Practice your first note by playing "One Note Reggae." Practice your "toe-tap" with a steady beat on the quarter notes.

2. Show your family and/or friends the graphic *Butterfly II* and explain the groupings of "4." Perform "One Note Reggae" for your family and/or friends and read *Butterfly II* as your music.

3. Create your own graphic that represents patterns of quarter notes and quarter rests.

4. Practice Stroke Dexterity Exercises #1–6.

The Art of Playing Triangle, Wood Block and Cowbell

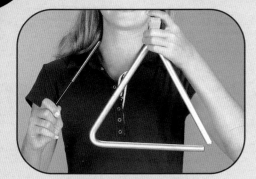

Setup Procedure

1. The triangle should be suspended from a triangle clip with a thin piece of nylon line. Hold the clip comfortably in the hand so that your fingers can be used for muffling.

2. The triangle may be clipped to the music stand to accommodate quick instrument changes or during rapid passages played with two beaters.

Setup Procedure

1. Hold the wood block in one hand to form a trough underneath. The wood block should rest lightly in the hand so that it makes the most resonant sound possible.

2. A rubber mallet will give a full resonant sound and a snare drum stick will produce a lighter sound.

Setup Procedure

1. Hold the cowbell in one hand to form a trough underneath. The cowbell should rest lightly in the hand so that it makes the most resonant sound possible.

2. The basic matched grip for the stick or mallet is the same as that for snare drum.

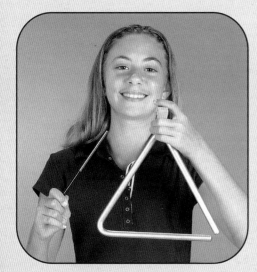

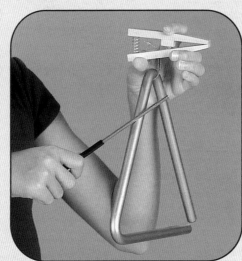

Ready Position

- Hold the triangle at eye level so that you can easily watch the triangle, the conductor, and the music.

- Hold the triangle beater near the end.

Play Position

- Strike the triangle on the side directly opposite the open end or on the bottom.

- Rolls are produced by rapidly moving the beater between the sides of one of the closed corners.

- Play with a shorter stroke near the tip of the beater for a soft, delicate sound.

- Play with a longer stroke near the center of the beater for a louder, more colorful sound.

- A good triangle has a multitude of playing areas that will yield a variety of tones. Experiment with different playing areas and different size beaters to become familiar with all the sounds available.

Damp Position

- Dampen with the fingers after the stroke is made to control the amount of sustain.

The Art of Playing Triangle, Wood Block and Cowbell

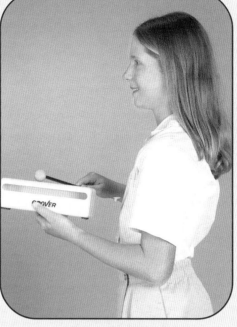

Ready Position

- Hold the wood block at eye level so that you can easily watch the block, the conductor, and the music.

- The basic matched grip for the stick or mallet is the same as that for snare drum.

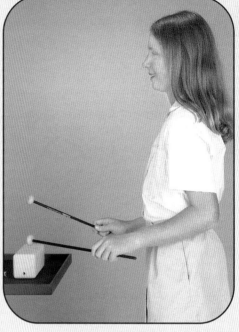

Play Position

- Using a wrist stroke similar to playing the snare drum, strike the block in the center over the open slit.

- Experiment with the playing area to find the exact "sweet spot" of the wood block.

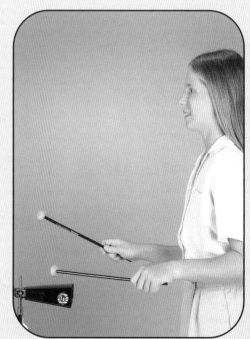

Play Position

- For quick instrument changes or rapid passages that require two sticks, place the wood block on a padded surface or suspended from a stand.

Ready Position

- Hold the cowbell at eye level so that you can easily watch the cowbell, the conductor, and the music.

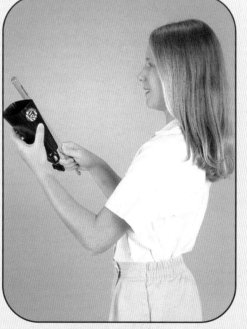

Play Position

- Using a wrist stroke similar to playing the snare drum, strike the cowbell above the open end with the butt of a snare drum stick or a rubber mallet.

- Play near the closed end for a brighter, drier sound.

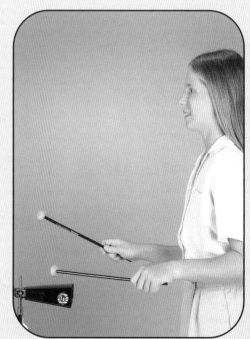

Play Position

- For quick instrument changes or rapid passages that require two sticks, place the cowbell on a padded surface or suspended from a stand.

Creative Tools of Music

Critique—an evaluation of the quality of a performance

Fermata—hold the note (or rest) longer than the note value

Intonation—the accuracy of pitch or pitch relationships in the performance of music

Ledger Lines—short lines placed above or below the staff for pitches beyond the range of the staff

Rest—a silent unit of time.

Soli—a line of music played by a small group of instruments

Tutti—all play

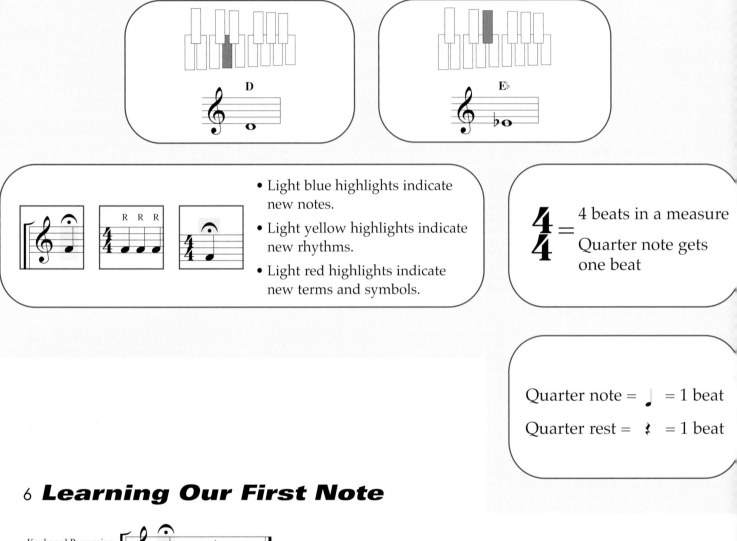

- Light blue highlights indicate new notes.
- Light yellow highlights indicate new rhythms.
- Light red highlights indicate new terms and symbols.

$$\frac{4}{4} = \begin{array}{l} \text{4 beats in a measure} \\ \text{Quarter note gets one beat} \end{array}$$

Quarter note = ♩ = 1 beat

Quarter rest = 𝄽 = 1 beat

6 *Learning Our First Note*

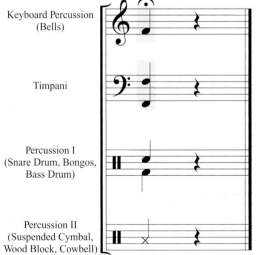

Keyboard Percussion (Bells)

Timpani

Percussion I (Snare Drum, Bongos, Bass Drum)

Percussion II (Suspended Cymbal, Wood Block, Cowbell)

7 Quarter Note Rock CD :9

8 Fermata Warm-Up CD :10

9 More Quarters CD :11

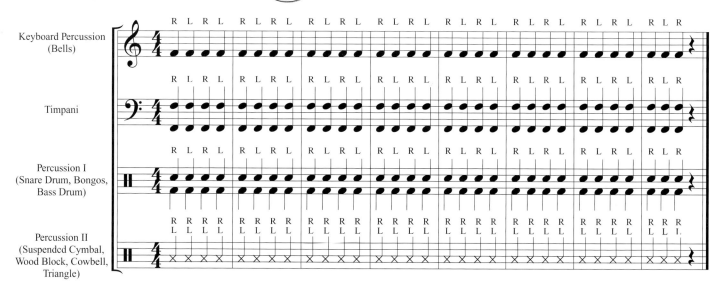

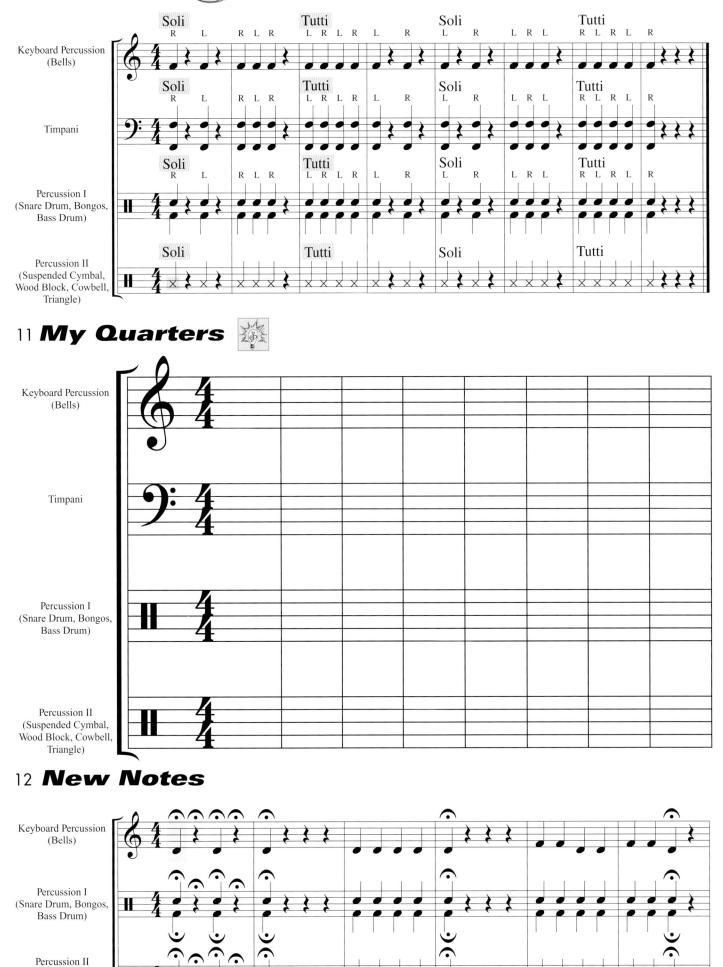

10 *Soli Jam* CD :12

11 **My Quarters**

12 **New Notes**

Go to the top of the next page

12 New Notes, continued

13 *El Toro* CD :13

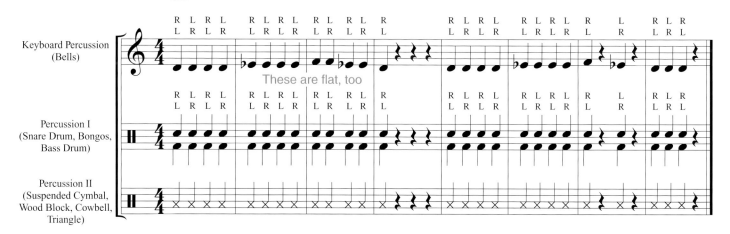

These are flat, too

Band @ Home

LESSON 1

1. Practice "More Quarters" for our next lesson. This exercise will help you develop your music reading skills.

2. Practice Stroke Dexterity Exercises #1–#8. Create your own version of a dexterity exercise and notate the pattern using "L" and "R."

LESSON 2

1. Schedule a consistent, daily time for practice in a quiet place so you are not distracted and can focus entirely on your music.

2. Practice "New Notes." This exercise introduces two new notes for your instrument. Notice the fingering chart in your book for the new notes.

3. Play "New Notes" for your family to show them what you have been learning.

4. Compose your own piece on the line entitled "My Quarters" in your book. Use any combination of quarter notes and quarter rests on your first note for the eight-measure composition. Be prepared to perform your composition in our next class.

5. Review Stroke Dexterity Exercises #1–#8.

6. Practice the Single Alternating Stroke at different speeds, keeping the strike motion as even as possible.

LESSON 3

1. Practice "Mixing the Three" in Unit 5.

2. Review Stroke Dexterity Exerciese #1–#8.

3. Practice the Single Alternating Stroke. (Look at the "Breakdown"*.) Start slowly and gradually increase in speed. Then, gradually decrease the speed to your starting point.

4. Explore www.band-expressions.com to find out more information about music and your instrument.

* Single Alternating Stroke "Breakdown"

——————— 60 seconds ———————

R L R L etc.

Creative Tools of Music

Canon—a technique to compose music in which the melody is introduced in one voice and echoed by another voice

Roll—an even, sustained sound on a percussion instrument

Solo—a performance by one person playing alone, with or without accompaniment

Roll Base—the rhythmic pattern that serves as the foundation for each roll stroke

Rudiment

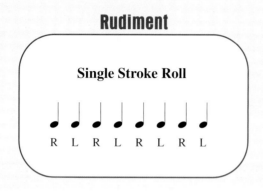

Single Stroke Roll

R L R L R L R L

14 *Mixing the Three*

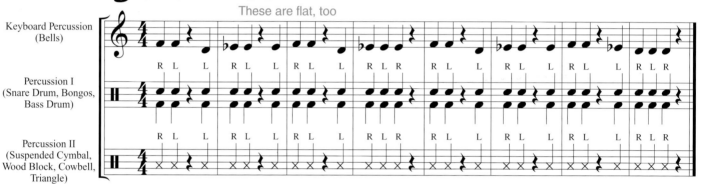

Keyboard Percussion (Bells)

These are flat, too

Percussion I (Snare Drum, Bongos, Bass Drum)

Percussion II (Suspended Cymbal, Wood Block, Cowbell, Triangle)

15 *Solo Rock* CD :14

Keyboard Percussion (Bells)

These are flat, too   Solo   tutti

Percussion I (Snare Drum, Bongos, Bass Drum)

Solo tutti
R R R R L L L   R R R   L L L   R R R   L L L   R R R R L L L

Percussion II (Suspended Cymbal, Wood Block, Cowbell, Triangle)

Solo tutti
Solo tutti Solo
tutti

16 *Creative Expression*

17 Going the Distance

18 Hymnsong CD :15

19 Putting It Together

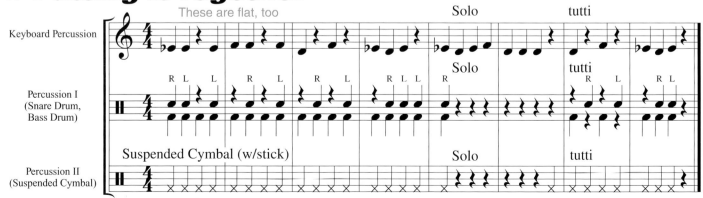

UNIT 5

20 Round and Round We Go

Keyboard Percussion (Bells) — *This is flat, too*

Percussion I (Snare Drum, Bass Drum)

Percussion II (Suspended Cymbal, Wood Block, Triangle)

Keybd. Perc.

Perc. I

Perc. II

21 Canon Roll

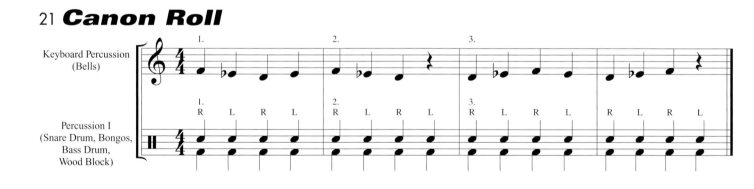

Keyboard Percussion (Bells)

Percussion I (Snare Drum, Bongos, Bass Drum, Wood Block)

Creative Tools Notation

Band @ Home

LESSON 1

1. Remember—it is important to follow our daily practice routine.

2. Practice "Going the Distance." This challenging exercise reviews what we have already learned.

3. Review Stroke Dexterity Exercises #1–#8.

4. Practice the Single Alternating Stroke. Start slowly, gradually increase to your top speed, maintain evenness in the sound, and gradually decrease the speed back to the starting point.

LESSON 2

1. Practice "Putting it Together." This selection reviews what we have learned to this point.

2. Practice Stroke Dexterity Exercise #1–#8.

3. Practice the Single Alternating Stroke, gradually increasing speed and slowing down again. Try gradually varying the stick heights (slow/low to fast/high to slow/low).

LESSON 3

1. Compose and teach a family member a canon using body percussion.

2. Be prepared to teach your canon to the band in our next lesson.

3. On the "Creative Tools Notation" line, practice drawing your clef, time signature, barlines, quarter notes and rests, a fermata, and a final barline.

4. Review Stroke Dexterity Exercises #1–#8.

5. Practice the Single Stroke Roll. Start slowly, gradually increase speed, maintain evenness, and gradually slow down again. Gradually vary the stick heights.

Creative Tools of Music

Balance—all parts played and heard equally

Duet—a piece of music with two interacting parts

Harmony—the result of two or more tones sounded at the same time

Key—the tonality of a piece of music

Key Signature—flats or sharps placed at the beginning of the staff that indicate which notes are to be altered throughout the piece

March—music for a parade or procession

Musical Line—direction or shape of a musical thought or idea

Unison—all performers play the same note

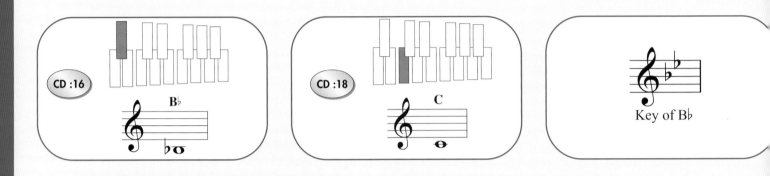

22 *Three Note Warm-Up*

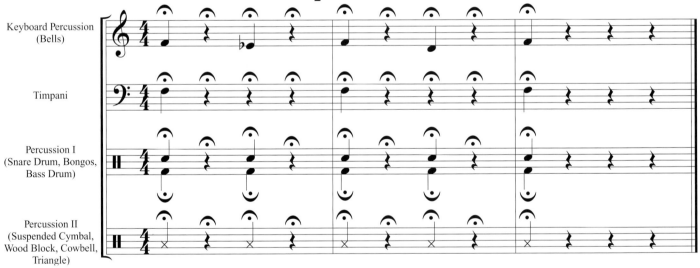

23 Woodchopper's Ball CD :17

Words and Music by
JOE BISHOP and WOODY HERMAN

24 Two for the Show (Duet)

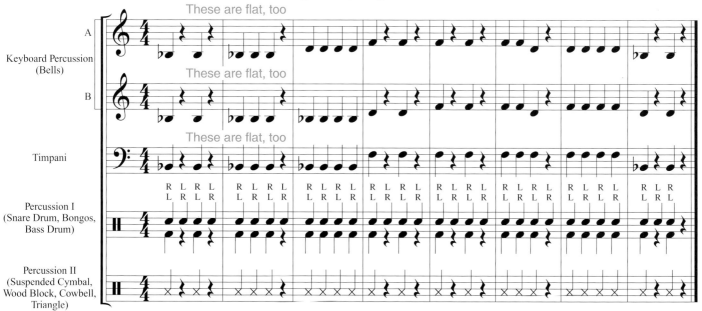

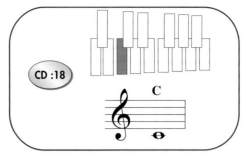

CD :18

25 *Two Tone Workout*

These are flat, too

Keyboard Percussion (Bells)

Percussion I (Snare Drum, Bongos, Bass Drum)

Percussion II (Suspended Cymbal, Wood Block, Cowbell, Triangle)

26 *Woodchopper's Ball* CD :19
(C Version)

Words and Music by
JOE BISHOP and WOODY HERMAN

Keyboard Percussion (Bells)

Percussion I (Snare Drum, Bongos, Bass Drum)

Percussion II (Suspended Cymbal, Wood Block, Cowbell, Triangle)

Keybd. Perc.

Perc. I

Perc. II

UNIT 6

27 A "Rock" Nophobia (Duet)
(The Eentsy Weentsy Spider)

Traditional, U.S.A.

29

28 Heroes March (Duet) CD :20

29 Balance Our Sound (Duet)

30 Ode to Joy (Duet) CD :21

LUDWIG VAN BEETHOVEN, Germany

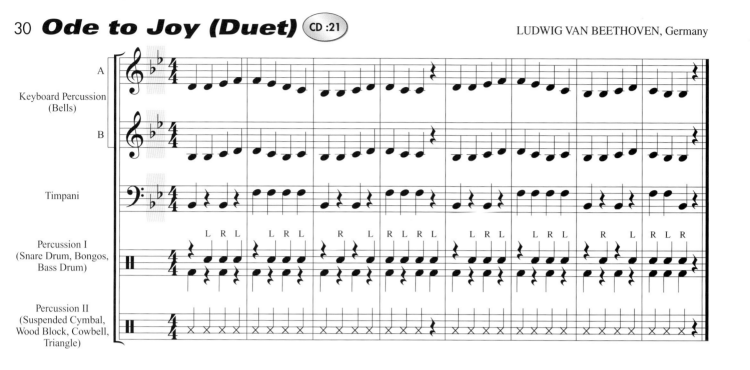

Keyboard Percussion (Bells)

Timpani

Percussion I (Snare Drum, Bongos, Bass Drum)

Percussion II (Suspended Cymbal, Wood Block, Cowbell, Triangle)

Band Home

LESSON 1

1. Practice playing the new note we learned today.

2. Perform "Woodchopper's Ball" with the accompaniment CD for your family and friends.

3. Practice Stroke Dexterity Exercises #1–#8.

LESSON 2

1. Play the new note for your family. Demonstrate your ability to hold and control steady long tones/beats.

2. Play 'Heroes March' with the CD accompaniment for your family and friends.

3. Practice Stroke Dexterity Exercises #9–#11.

LESSON 3

1. Practice Stroke Dexterity Exercises #9–#11.

2. Perform "Ode to Joy" with the accompaniment track for your family and friends.

3. Explore www.band-expressions.com to discover more information about music and your instrument.

Creative Tools of Music

Chorale—a slow, "hymn-like" composition

Composer—a person who writes music

Phrase—a musical sentence or statement

Repeat sign—symbol that indicates to go back and play the section of music again

John Williams

One of the most popular and successful American orchestral composers of the modern age, John Williams is the winner of five Academy Awards, 17 Grammys, three Golden Globes, and two Emmys. Mr. Williams has composed the music and served as music director for nearly eighty movies, including "Jaws;" "E.T.: The Extra-Terrestrial;" "Hook;" the "Indiana Jones;" trilogy and the "Star Wars" series. He is the Laureate Conductor of the Boston Pops Orchestra, which he conducted for 13 years and currently holds the title of Artist-in-Residence at Tanglewood, Massachusetts. He may be best known for the music he has written for the Olympics, including the well-known "Olympic Fanfare."

Multiple Bounce Stroke

Whole note = o = 4 counts

Whole rest = ▬ = 4 counts

Half note = ♩ = 2 counts

Half rest = ▬ = 2 counts

31 *Echo Warm-Up*

32 *Whole Lotta Fun*

33 *Half the Time*

34 *Thanksgiving Song*

Folk Song, England

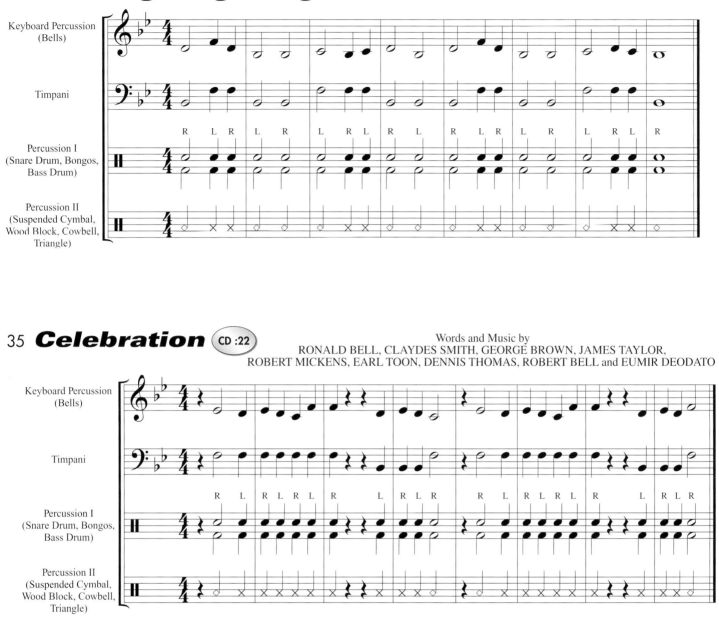

35 *Celebration* CD :22

Words and Music by
RONALD BELL, CLAYDES SMITH, GEORGE BROWN, JAMES TAYLOR,
ROBERT MICKENS, EARL TOON, DENNIS THOMAS, ROBERT BELL and EUMIR DEODATO

36 *Whole Note Warm-Up*

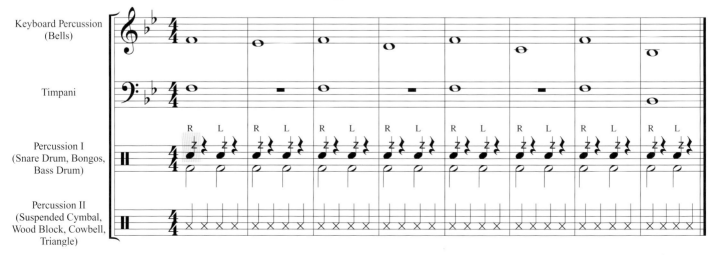

37 Phrase Phun

38 OK Chorale (Duet)

39 All Through the Night

Folk Song, Wales

Band @ Home

LESSON 1

1. Practice Stroke Dexterity Exercises #9–#11.

2. Practice "Celebration" with the accompaniment.

LESSON 2

1. Practice the melodies we learned today.

2. Practice Multiple Bounce Strokes and Stroke Dexterity Exercises #12–#13.

UNIT 8 IS PRESENTED BY YOUR TEACHER

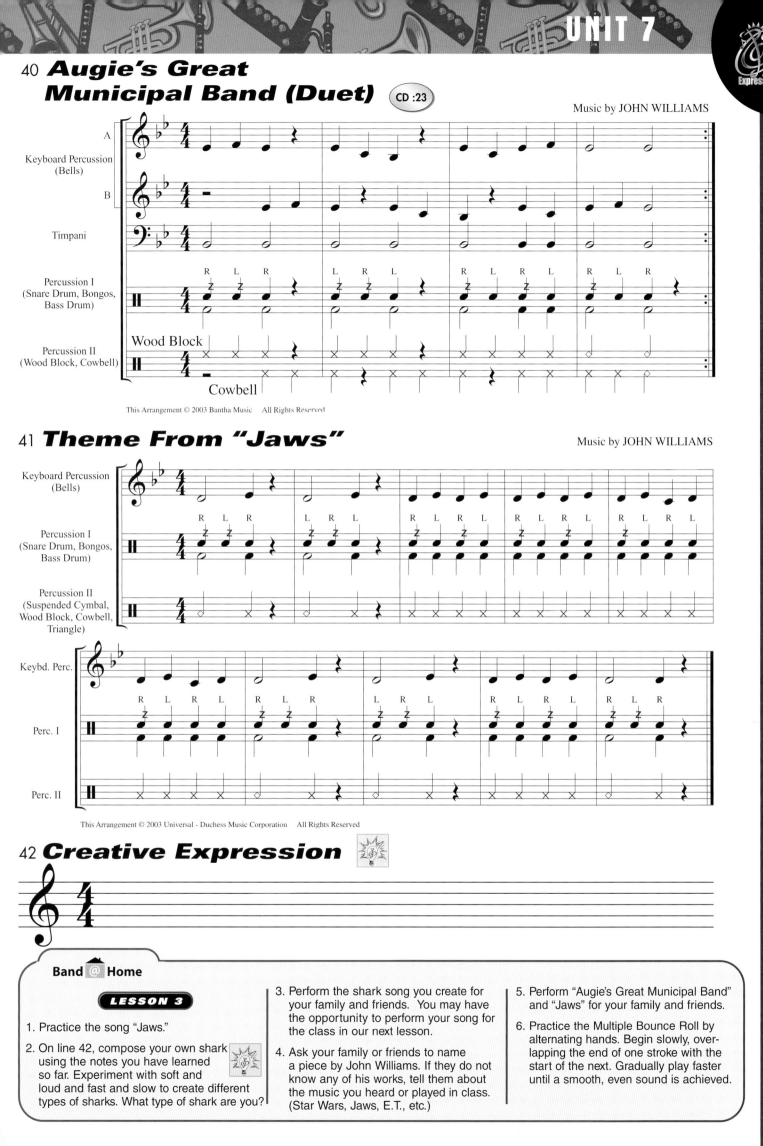

40 **Augie's Great Municipal Band (Duet)** CD :23

Music by JOHN WILLIAMS

This Arrangement © 2003 Bantha Music   All Rights Reserved

41 *Theme From "Jaws"*

Music by JOHN WILLIAMS

This Arrangement © 2003 Universal - Duchess Music Corporation   All Rights Reserved

42 *Creative Expression*

Band @ Home

LESSON 3

1. Practice the song "Jaws."

2. On line 42, compose your own shark using the notes you have learned so far. Experiment with soft and loud and fast and slow to create different types of sharks. What type of shark are you?

3. Perform the shark song you create for your family and friends. You may have the opportunity to perform your song for the class in our next lesson.

4. Ask your family or friends to name a piece by John Williams. If they do not know any of his works, tell them about the music you heard or played in class. (Star Wars, Jaws, E.T., etc.)

5. Perform "Augie's Great Municipal Band" and "Jaws" for your family and friends.

6. Practice the Multiple Bounce Roll by alternating hands. Begin slowly, overlapping the end of one stroke with the start of the next. Gradually play faster until a smooth, even sound is achieved.

Creative Tools of Music

Anacrusis—one or more notes that occur as a lead-in to the first full measure

Dynamics—musical performace levels of loud and soft

Sight-reading—reading and performing a piece of music for the first time

Subdivide—dividing a note into smaller sections or fractions

Dynamic Markings

p	the symbol for piano, meaning to play soft
mp	the symbol for mezzo piano, meaning to play medium soft
mf	the symbol for mezzo forte, meaning to play medium loud
f	the symbol for forte, meaning to play loud

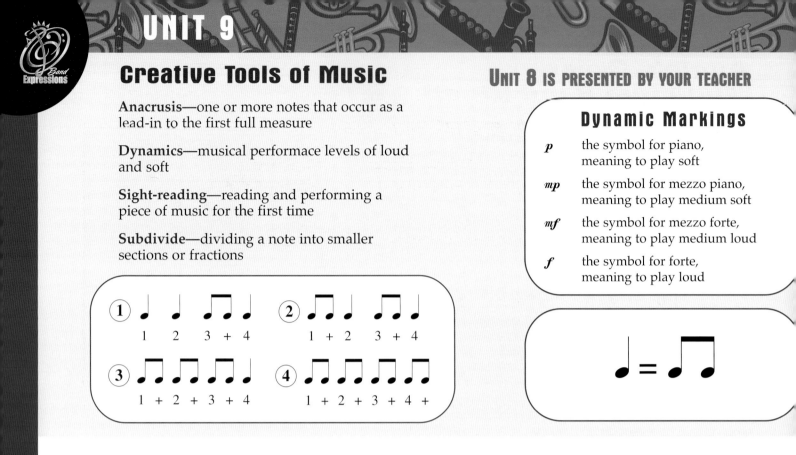

43 Playing the Phrase CD :24

44 Reading the Eighths

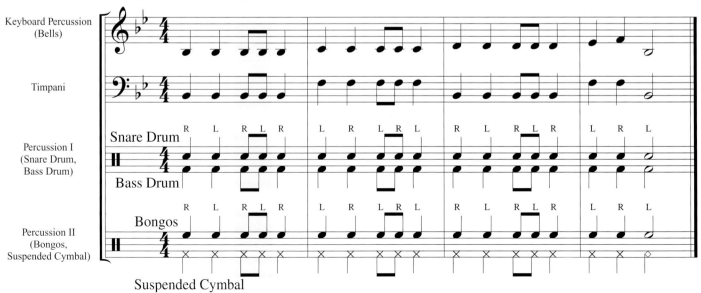

45 *Three Pairs and a Caterpillar*

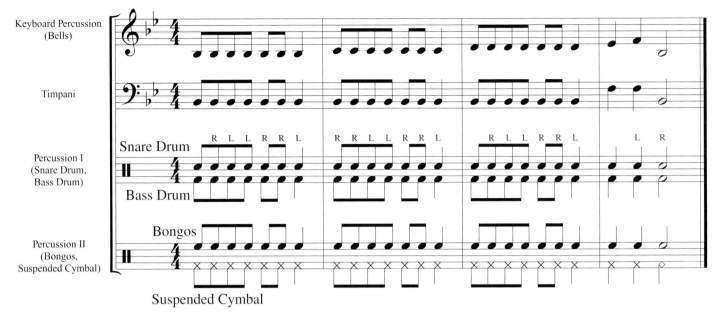

46 *Rain, Rain Go Away* CD :25

Traditional

47 Creative Expression

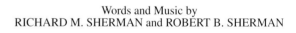

48 Feel the Force! CD :26

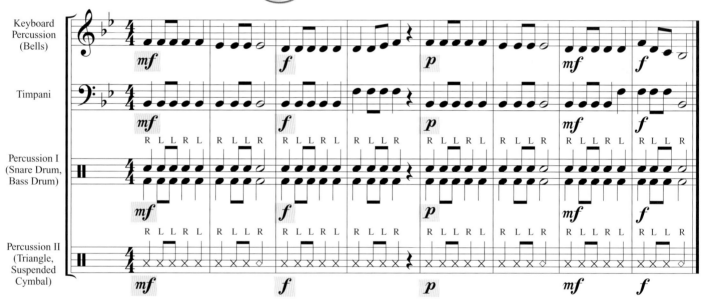

49 Chitty, Chitty Bang Bang CD :27

Words and Music by
RICHARD M. SHERMAN and ROBERT B. SHERMAN

Go to the top of the next page.

Chitty, Chitty Bang Bang, continued

50 *Arre, Mi Burrito!* CD :28

Folk Song, Latin America

51 *Juba*

African-American Folk Song, U.S.A.

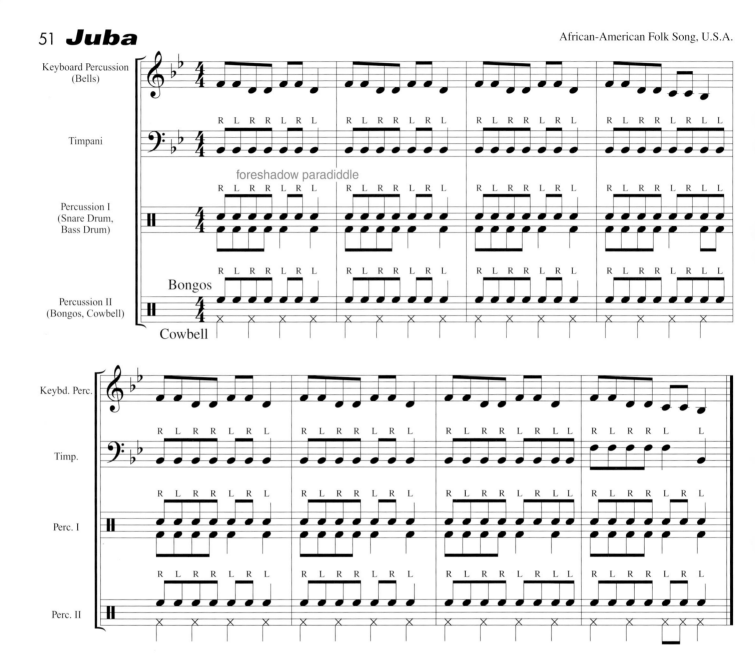

52 **Mary's New Groove** CD :29

Traditional, U.S.A.

53 Duerme Pronto CD :30

Folk Song, Spain

54 Long Legged Sailor

Traditional, Folk Song

55 Bang the Drum All Day CD :31
(I Don't Want to Work)

Words and Music by TODD RUNDGREN

Keyboard Percussion (Bells)

mf

I don't want to work, just want to bang on the drum all day.

Timpani

mf

Percussion I (Snare Drum, Bass Drum)

mf

Percussion II (Triangle, Suspended Cymbal)

Triangle

Susp. Cym.

mf

Keybd. Perc.

I don't want to work, just want to bang on the drum all day.

Timp.

Perc. I

Perc. II

Band @ Home

LESSON 1

1. Remember to follow your warm-up procedure. Play one of your favorite songs from earlier in the book to complete your warm-up.

2. On the Creative Expression line, create and notate four measures of eighth note and quarter note combinations using any pitch you can read and play. Clap, count, and play your composition.

3. Practice "Rain Rain, Go Away" with the CD accompaniment.

4. Practice Stroke Dexterity Exercises #12–#13 and the Multiple Bounce Roll.

LESSON 2

1. Play the new song "Juba."

2. Draw dynamic symbols (piano, forte, mezzo forte, and mezzo piano) where you think they belong.

3. Play "Juba" with the dynamics you have added. Be prepared to play this in class next time.

4. Memorize "Rain, Rain Go Away."

5. Practice Stroke Dexterity Exercises #12–#13 and the Multiple Bounce Roll.

LESSON 3

1. Teach the words to "Bang the Drum All Day" to your family and friends. Invite them to perform "Bang the Drum All Day" with you and the accompaniment track.

2. Review Stroke Dexterity Exercises #1–#13 and the Multiple Bounce Roll.

Creative Tools of Music

Melody—a series of musical tones that form a recognizable phrase

Ostinato—a repeated melodic or rhythmic pattern

Slur—a curved line placed above or below two or more notes to indicate that they are to be performed smooth and connected

Tempo—the speed of the beat

Tie—a curved line connecting two notes of the same pitch and played as if they were one

Tie   Slur

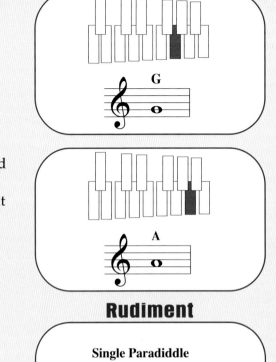

G

A

Rudiment

Single Paradiddle

R L R R L R L L

PORTRAIT

Percy Grainger
(1882–1961)

An Australian composer, he lived from 1882 to 1961. His music is based on folk songs he collected from throughout the British Isles. He used a phonograph to record men and women singing the songs that were passed down to them from their parents and grandparents. In his arrangements of these folk songs for band, he tried to keep the phrasing as close to the original vocal performance as possible.

56 *New Vistas*

Keyboard Percussion (Bells)   *mf*

Timpani   *mf*

Percussion I (Suspended Cymbal)   *mf*

Percussion II (Triangle)   *mf*

57 *Claire de Lune*   CD :32

Folk Song, France

Keyboard Percussion (Bells)   *mf*

Timpani   *mf*

Percussion I (Triangle)   *mf*

Percussion II (Suspended Cymbal)   *mf*

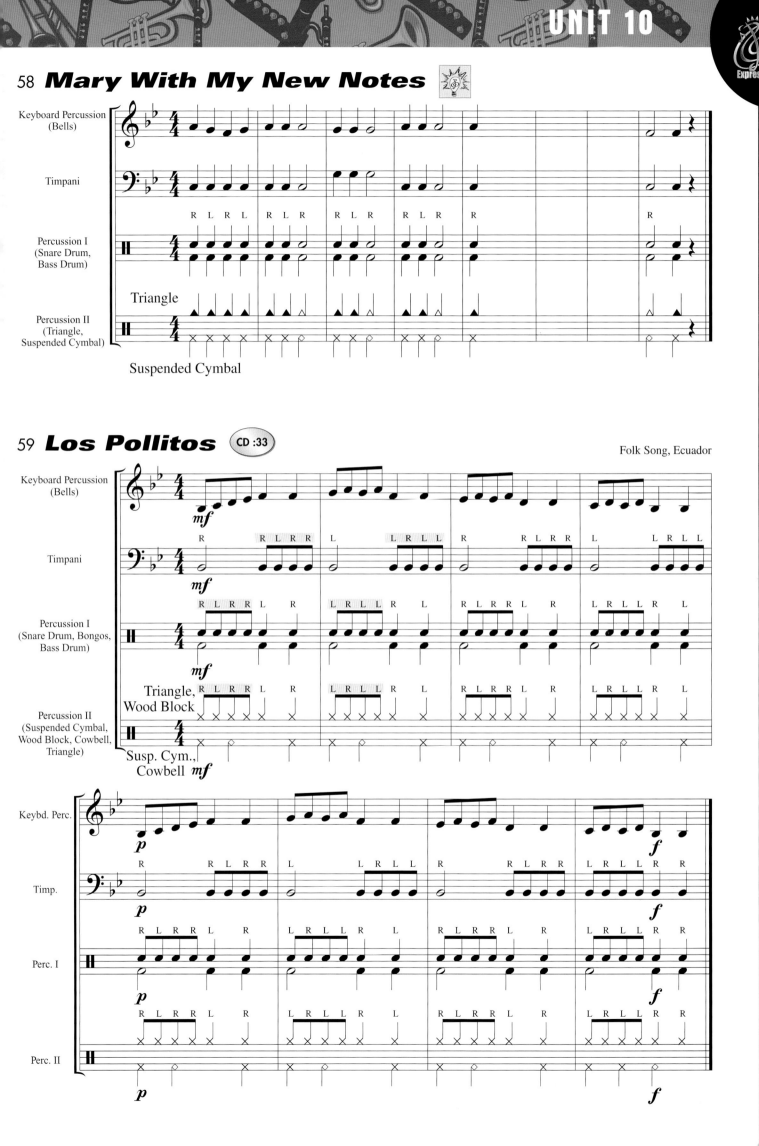

60 **When the Saints Go Marching In** CD :34

JAMES M. BLACK and
KATHERINE E. PURVIS, U.S.A.

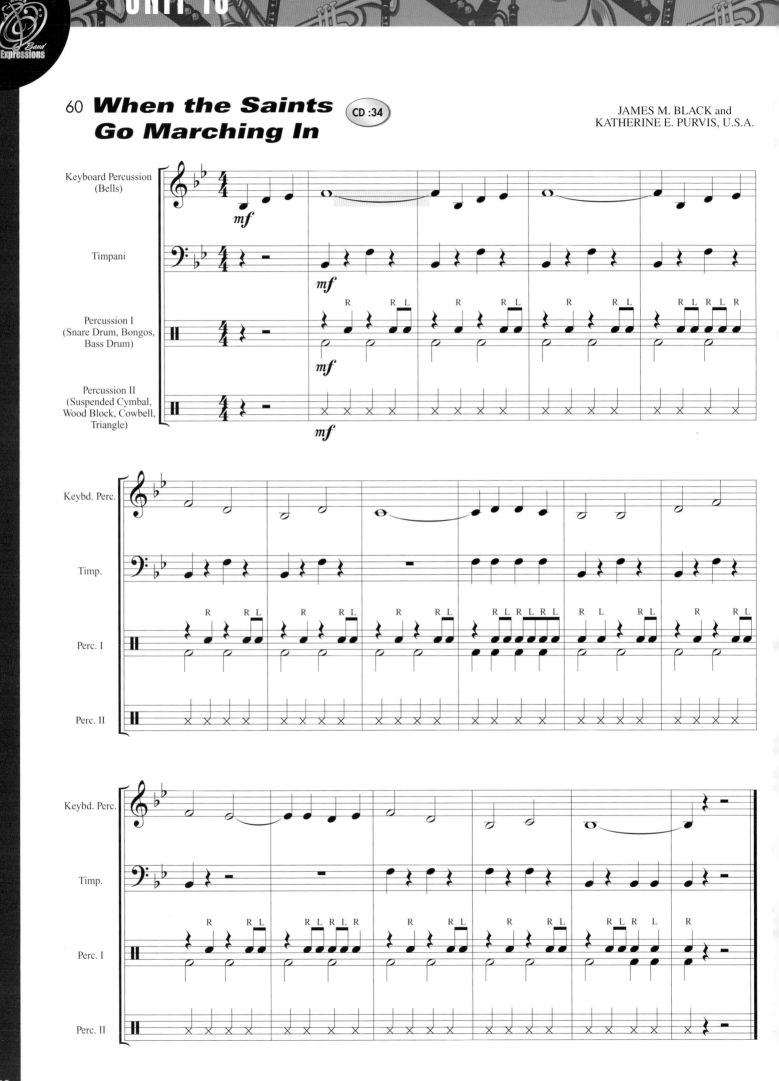

1 Catch a Falling Star

CD :35

Words and Music by
PAUL VANCE and LEE POCKRISS

Keyboard Percussion
(Bells)

Timpani

Percussion I
(Snare Drum,
Bass Drum)

Triangle

Percussion II
(Triangle,
Suspended Cymbal)

Kybd. Perc.

Timp.

Perc. I

Perc. II

Suspended Cymbal

2 Sarasponda

Folk Song, Holland

Keyboard
Percussion
(Bells)

Ostinato

Timpani

Ostinato

Percussion I
(Snare Drum,
Bass Drum)

Ostinato

Triangle

Percussion II
(Triangle,
Suspended
Cymbal)

Suspended Cymbal

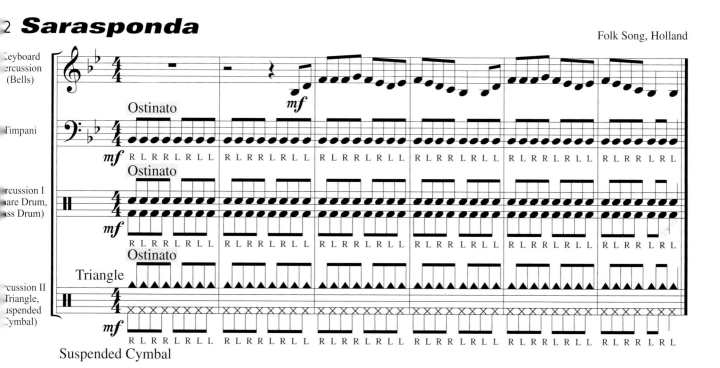

63 Shepherd's Hey CD :36

Country Dance, England

Triangle

Suspended Cymbal

Rudiment Review Exercises

SINGLE STROKE ROLL

R L R L R L R L R L R L R L R L

MULTIPLE BOUNCE ROLL

R L R L R L R L R L R L R L R L

PARADIDDLE

R L R R L R L L R L R R L R L L

Rudiment "Breakdown"

—— 60 seconds ——

Band @ Home

LESSON 1

1. Complete "Mary With My New Notes" by notating the missing melody. We will play our completed song in our next lesson.

2. Practice playing "Claire De Lune" with the accompaniment track.

3. Practice Stroke Dexterity Exercises #14–#15 and the Multiple Bounce Roll.

LESSON 2

1. Practice "Los Pollitos," "When the Saints Go Marching In," and "Catch a Falling Star" at different tempi.

2. Explain and play for someone at home the difference between a tie and a slur.

3. Revise "Mary With My New Notes" looking for:

   • Straight note flags
   • Neatly written note heads
   • Correct notes
   • Evenly spaced notes

4. Add the following to your composition:

   • New appropriate words
   • Dynamics

5. Be prepared to share your composition with the band.

LESSON 3

1. Create a one measure rhythmic ostinato to accompany "Mary With My New Notes".

2. Your ostinato should be on our first note (F) using any combination of quarter and eighth notes and quarter rests.

3. Remember that an ostinato is a repeated pattern.

4. Review Stroke Dexterity Exercises #1–#15 and the Multiple Bounce Roll.

5. Practice the "Rudiment Review Exercises." Start slowly and gradually increase speed, keeping a steady and even rhythm.

Creative Tools of Music

> **Accent**—play the note with more emphasis

Chord—three or more tones sounded at the same time

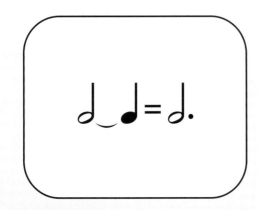 **Dot**—increases the value of the preceding note or rest by one half

1st and 2nd Endings—play the first ending the first time only and the second ending the second time

Time Signature—a symbol placed at the beginning of the staff with the top number indicating that there are 3 beats per measure, and the bottom number indicating a quarter note, which equals one beat

$\frac{3}{4}$

$\frac{3}{4}$ Conducting Pattern

PORTRAIT

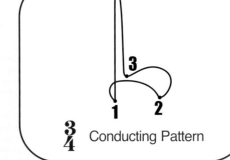

Gustav Holst
(1874–1934)

Gustav Holst was born in Cheltenham, England in 1874 and began composing while at Cheltenham Grammar School. While studying at the Royal College of Music, he met Ralph Vaughan Williams, another famous composer, and the two were close friends, always playing drafts of their newest compositions to each other. Holst was a teacher his whole life and because of a heavy and demanding teaching load, it took him many years to write his most famous work, "The Planets" (1914-1916). Despite his initial training at the Royal College of Music, Holst was largely self-taught as a composer, mostly learning by experience. He was an intense nationalist, and after his rejection from the Royal military because of his bad eyesight, he became a conductor of the military band, and toured much of Europe supporting the British through music. Some of his most well-known pieces include "Moorside Suite," "Suite in E♭," "Suite in F," and "The Planets."

64 *Three at a Time*

65 Batman Theme CD :37

Words and Music by NEAL HEFTI
paradiddle sticking

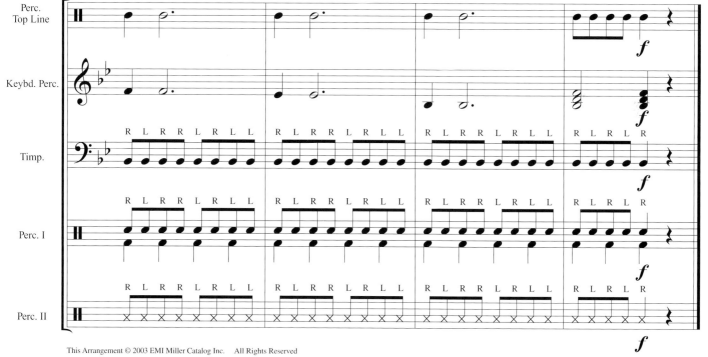

66 *Around Her Neck*
She Wore a Yellow Ribbon

Traditional, U.S.A.

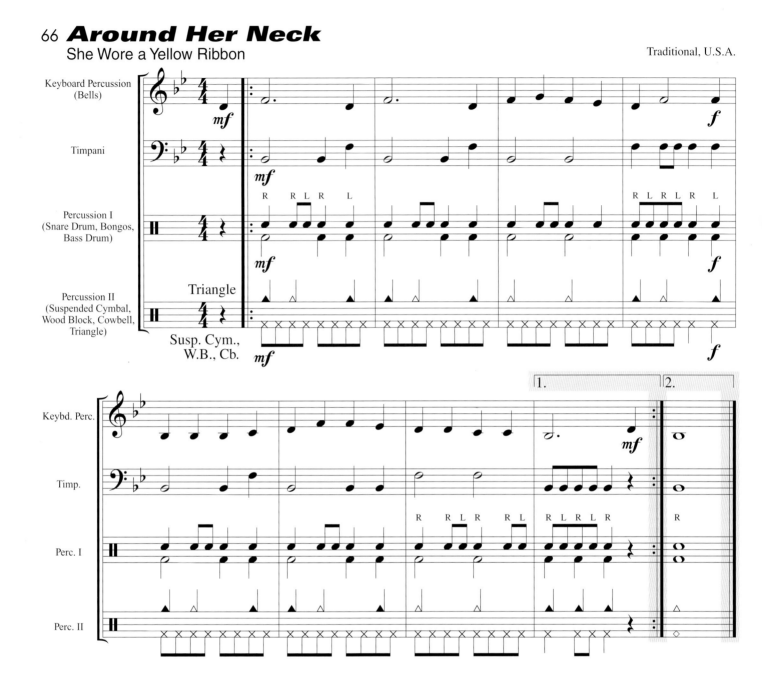

67 *Shusti Fidli* CD :38

Folk Song, Czechoslovakia

68 *Change the Drum* CD :39

69 *Oh Dear, What Can the Matter Be?* CD :40

Folk Song, England/Scotland

70 *In the Bleak Midwinter* CD :41

GUSTAV HOLST, England

Band @ Home

LESSON 1

1. After warming up properly, practice "Batman Theme" and "Around Her Neck."

2. Perform these songs for your family and friends. You may wish to ask your family if they remember "Batman Theme" from the classic television series.

3. Practice Stroke Dexterity Exercises #16–#17, the Multiple Bounce Roll, and the Paradiddle.

LESSON 2

1. Explain 3/4 time to one of your family members.

2. Ask them to count for you as you play "Shusti Fidli."

3. Practice conducting each exercise before performing.

4. Practice Stroke Dexterity Exercises #16–#17, the Multiple Bounce Roll, and the Paradiddle.

LESSON 3

1. Create and notate a new 8-count accent pattern. Be prepared to notate the pattern on the board during our next lesson for the band to play.

2. Practice "Oh Dear, What Can the Matter Be?" and "In the Bleak Midwinter."

3. Teach one of your family members how to conduct in a 3/4 time signature. Ask the family member to conduct as you play "Oh Dear, What Can the Matter Be?"

4. Practice Stroke Dexterity Exercises #1–#20, the Multiple Bounce Roll, and the Paradiddle.

The Art of Playing Sleigh Bells

Setup Procedure

- Sleigh bells should be placed on a padded surface to make their pickup and replacement as silent as possible.

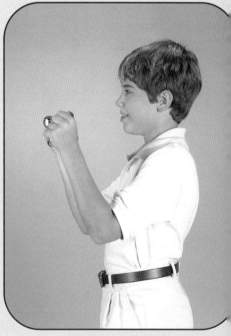

Ready Position

- Hold the handle of the sleigh bells in one hand and the opposite end of the sleigh bells in the other hand so that the bells are parallel to the floor.

Play Position

- To perform specific rhythms, shake the sleigh bells in the rhythm indicated.

Play Position

- To perform a roll, hold the sleigh bells parallel to the floor at both ends and rapidly shake them.

The Art of Playing Tambourine

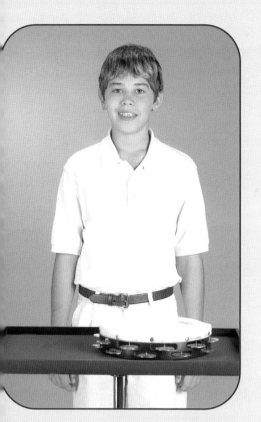

Setup Procedure

- The tambourine should be placed on a padded surface to make its pickup and replacement as silent as possible.

- Hold the tambourine firmly in one hand with your thumb placed on the head and your fingers wrapped around the shell.

Ready Position

- Hold the tambourine at eye level so that you can easily watch the tambourine, conductor, and the music.

- Clear articulation is achieved when the tambourine is held eye level, at a slight angle to the floor.

Play Position

- For a full sound, make a fist and strike the center of the head with your knuckles.

- For a softer sound, strike the head at the edge or on the rim with one or two of your fingertips. Move toward the center and add fingers as the volume increases.

- Experiment to find the areas on the head that produce the most jingle sound for each volume level.

Play Position

- Shake rolls should be performed by a quick rotation of the wrist with the tambourine in a vertical position. Most rolls will start and stop with a strike on the head.

Creative Tools of Music

Accidental—a sharp, flat or neutral, in a way not indicated in the key signatures

Concert pitch—the actual sounding pitch of a note played by an instrument

Introduction—a short section of music preceding the piece

Natural—this symbol cancels a previous sharp or flat sign; like a flat or sharp, it is used for the entire measure

Rock—a style of popular music that originated in America, characterized by a strong rhythmic beat and electronic instruments

Concert Pitch	F	D	E♭	B♭
C Instruments	F	D	E♭	B♭
B♭ Instruments	G	E	F	C
E♭ Instruments	D	B	C	G
F Instruments	C	A	B♭	F

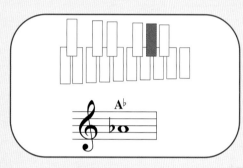

A♭

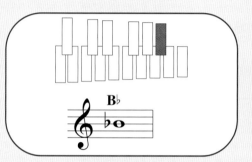

B♭

Key of E♭

Rudiment

Flam

L R   R L

The Flam is introduced in 73 March Flam.

71 Song in E Flat

Keyboard Percussion (Bells)

Timpani

Percussion I (Snare Drum, Bongos, Bass Drum)

Percussion II (Suspended Cymbal, Wood Block, Cowbell, Triangle)

Triangle, Susp. Cym.

Cowbell, Wood Block

72 *There's No One Exactly Like Me*

By BETTY ANN RAMSETH

73 March Flam CD :42

74 Happy Birthday to You! CD :43

Words and Music by
MILDRED J. HILL and PATTY S. HILL

Go to the top of the next page.

Happy Birthday to You!, continued

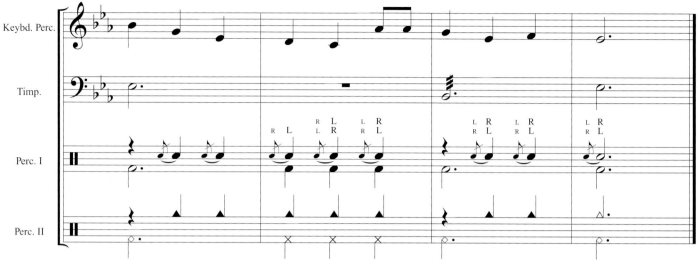

75 *Jingle Bells*   CD :44

J. PIERPONT, U.S.A.

76 Jingle Bell Rock CD :45

Words and Music by
JOE BEAL and JIM BOOTHE

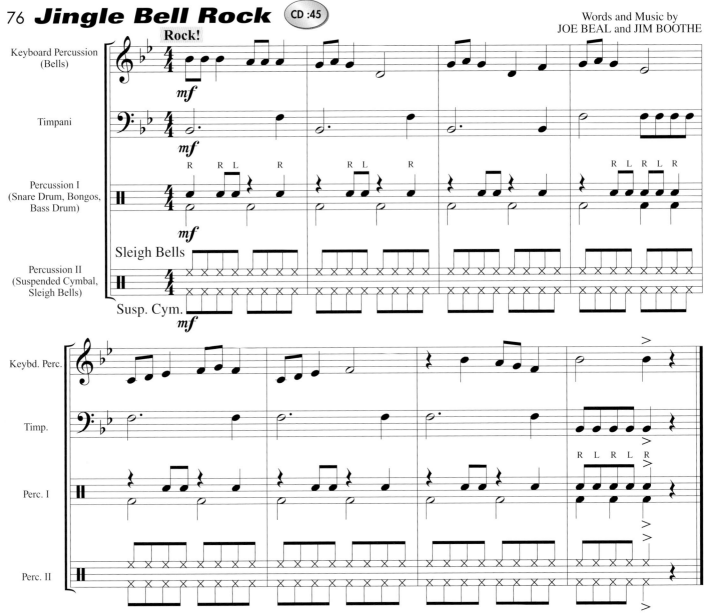

77 **_Sunrise, Sunset_** CD :46

Lyrics by SHELDON HARNICK
Music by JERRY BOCK

78 *Hine Ma Tov* (CD :47)

Folk Song, Israel

Band @ Home

LESSON 1

1. Practice "There's No One Exactly Like Me" and "Happy Birthday to You!"

2. Perform "Happy Birthday to You!" for your family and friends.

3. Practice the Flam, being sure to keep the grace note low and the main note high.

LESSON 2

1. Your warm-up should always include a review of Stroke Dexterity Exercises #1–#20 and the rudiments you have learned.

2. Practice "Jingle Bells" and "Jingle Bell Rock" alone and with the accompaniment tracks.

3. Memorize "Happy Birthday to You!"

LESSON 3

1. Warm-up on the Stroke Dexterity Exercises and the rudiments you have learned.

2. Practice playing concert pitches with a friend from band or while someone plays the concert pitches on the piano or keyboard.

Stroke Dexterity Exercises

1. R R R R   R R R R   L L L L   L L L L

2. R R R R   L L L L   R R R R   L L L L

3. R R R L   R R R L   R R R L   R R R L

4. L L L R   L L L R   L L L R   L L L R

5. R L L L   R L L L   R L L L   R L L L

6. L R R R   L R R R   L R R R   L R R R

7. R R L L   R R L L   R R L L   R R L L

8. R L R L   R L R L   R L R L   R L R L

9. R L R L   R R R R   L R L R   L L L L

10. R L R L   R L R R   R L R L   R L R R

11. L R L R   L R L L   L R L R   L R L L

12. R L R L   R R L L   R L R L   R R L L

13. L R L R   L L R R   L R L R   L L R R

14. R L R R   L L R R   L R L L   R R L L

15. R L R R   L R L L   R L R R   L R L L

16. R R L R   L L R L   R L R R   L R L L

17. R L L R   L R R L   R L L R   L R R L

18. R L R L   R L R R   L R L R   L R L L

19. R L R L   R R L R   L R L R   L L R L

20. R L R L   R L L R   L R L R   L R R L

The Art of Playing Maracas

Setup Procedure

- The maracas should be placed on a padded surface to make their pickup and replacement as silent as possible.

Ready Position

- Hold the maracas at chest level, parallel to the floor.

Play Position

- Make a quick downward wrist stroke in the air to produce a clear sound on the maracas.
- Rhythms are played using single alternating strokes.

Play Position

- Hold the maracas at chest level, perpendicular to the floor to play rolls.
- Rolls are played by using very fast, alternating wrist shakes.

The Art of Playing Tube Shaker

Setup Procedure

- 1. Tube shakers (also called ganza or chocallo) are found in a variety of sizes and can be constructed from metal, plastic, or wood. They are filled with any type of pellet including seeds, dry beans, shot, sand, rice, and gravel.
- 2. The tube shaker should be placed on a padded surface to make the pickup and replacement as silent as possible.

Ready Position

- Hold the tube shaker with one or both hands at eye level, parallel to the floor.

Play Position

- Make a sharp back-and-forth motion with the wrists and forearms to produce a clear sound on the tube shaker.
- A steady rhythm is created as the pellets strike the inside of the tube at opposite sides.

Play Position

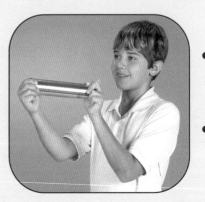

- Hold the tube shaker at chest level, parallel to the floor to play rolls.
- Rolls are played by using very fast, alternating wrist shakes.

The Art of Playing Xylophone

Please refer to pages 12-13, The Art of Playing Percussion

Xylophone

Creative Tools of Music

Balance—the dynamic strength and importance given to instruments/voices within a composition

Multiple Measure Rest—a symbol indicating more than one measure of rest

Rehearsal Numbers/Letters—markings above the staff that indicate specific locations in the music

Sight-reading—the playing of a piece of music for the first time

Style—how notes, rhythms, and articulations are treated in musical performance

Creative Tools of Music

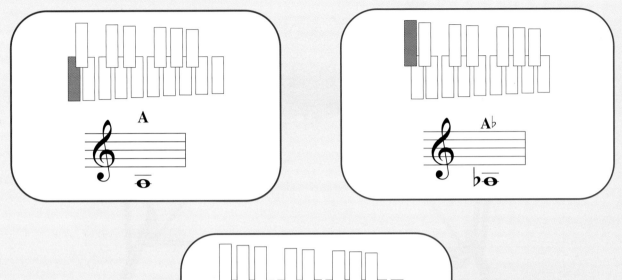

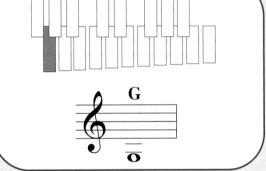

SIGHT-READING PROCEDURE MAP (SRPM)

1. Look at the title, composer, time signature, and key signature.

2. Look through the entire piece for the musical road map and for any key or time signature changes.

3. Follow along each line of music with your finger to be sure you know all of the notes and understand all of the rhythms and musical markings.

4. Count through the entire piece silently while tapping your foot.

5. Finger/airstick through the entire piece. Be sure to look at the words and symbols around the notes for all of the performance information.

6. Silently practice the difficult passages.

79 *Lotta Latin*

80 **Feliz Navidad** CD :48

Words and Music by JOSE FELICIANO
Arranged by MICHAEL STORY

Feliz Navidad - 2

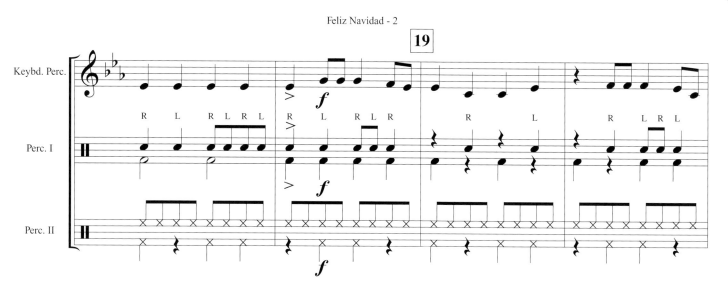

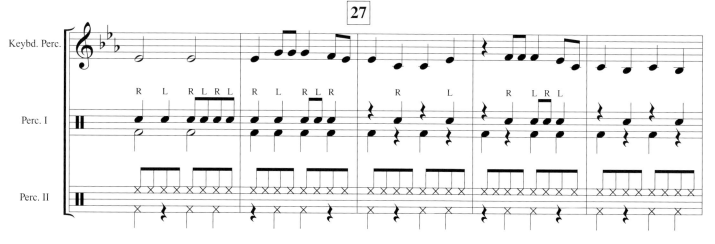

81 **Up on the Housetop** CD :49

BENJAMIN RUSSELL HANBY, U.S.A.
Arranged by MICHAEL STORY

Up on the Housetop - 2

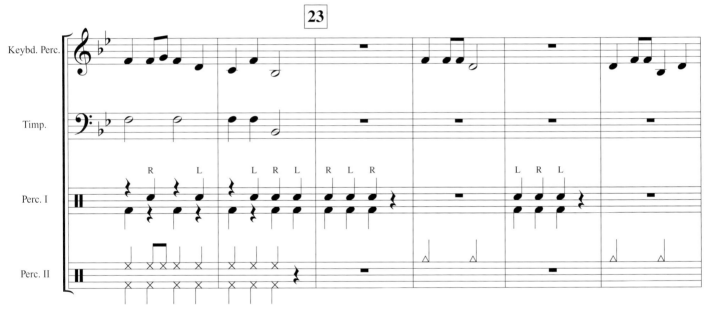

To avoid page turns, your music can be found on the following pages:

82 **Rock Warm-Up**

83 **Winter Wonderland** can be found on pages 74-75.

84 **Holiday Warm-Up**

85 **We Wish You a Merry Christmas** can be found on pages 76-77.

82 **Rock Warm-Up** can be found on page 72.

83 **Winter Wonderland** CD :50

Words by DICK SMITH
Music by FELIX BERNARD
Arranged by ROBERT W. SMITH

Winter Wonderland - 2

17

84 *Holiday Warm-Up* can be found on page 73.

84 **Holiday Warm-Up** can be found on page 73.

85 ## We Wish You a Merry Christmas

Traditional, England
Arranged by ROBERT W. SMITH

We Wish You a Merry Christmas - 2

86 Dynamic Warm-Up can be found on page 80.

86 **Dynamic Warm-Up** can be found on page 80.

87 *African Patapan* CD :51

Carol, France
Arranged by MICHAEL STORY

African Patapan - 2

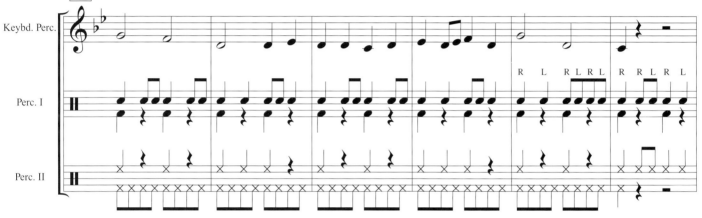

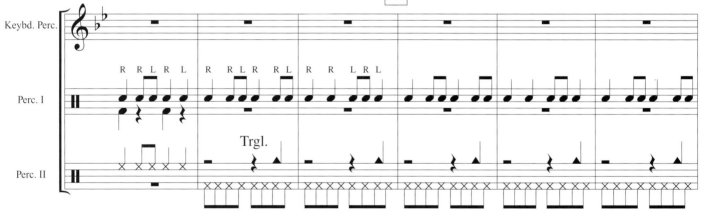

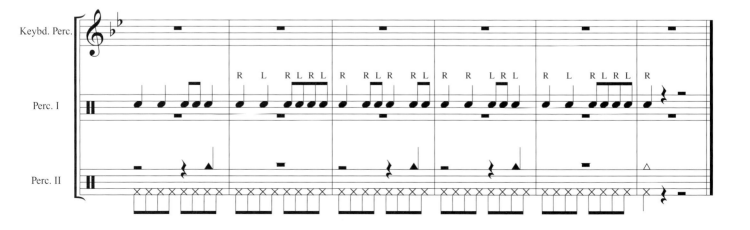

88 ***Concert Chorale*** can be found on the bottom of the next page.

85 **We Wish You a Merry Christmas** can be found on pages 76-7

86 Dynamic Warm-Up

87 **African Patapan** can be found on pages 78-79.

88 Concert Chorale

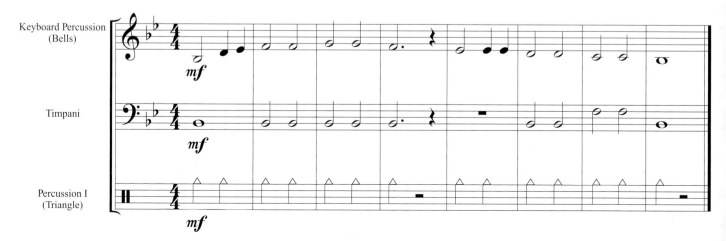

Auld Lang Syne (Solo)

Traditional, Scotland

mf

5

9

Jingle Bells (Solo)

J. PIERPONT, U.S.A.

mf

9

Band @ Home

UNIT 13

LESSON 1

1. Practice "Feliz Navidad."

2. Warm-up on Stroke Dexterity Exercises and the rudiments you have learned.

LESSON 2

1. Practice "Feliz Navidad" and "Up on the Housetop," considering the style for each piece.

2. Remember to isolate the more difficult passages, playing them slowly and gradually increasing the speed.

3. Record yourself playing your part on "Feliz Navidad." Write down what you discovered from critically listening to yourself play.

Band @ Home

UNIT 14

LESSON 1

1. Review all three of the concert pieces, striving for individual improvement.

2. Make a recording of your performance of each piece and turn it in at our next lesson. Your teacher will review your recording and provide feedback for improvement.

LESSON 2

1. Review all of the concert pieces we have learned so far. If you are having difficulty with particular sections of a piece, play the section slowly to improve before going on.

Band @ Home

UNIT 15

LESSON 1

1. Review all of the concert pieces.

LESSON 2

1. Polish your performance on all of the concert pieces and prepare all music, equipment, and concert attire.

2. Tell your family and friends the reporting time and concert time.

3. Practice the solo pieces, "Jingle Bells" and "Auld Lang Syne," and perform them for your family and friends.

The Art of Playing Güiro

Instrument and Parts

Setup Procedure

- The Güiro should be placed on a padded surface to make their pickup and replacement as silent as possible.

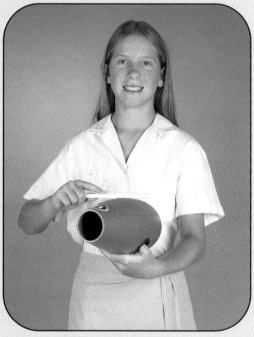

Ready Position

- Insert the thumb and middle finger into the holes cut into the bottom of the güiro. Hold the güiro at chest level, parallel to the floor.

- A tapered scraper works best to produce a variety of sounds and dynamics.

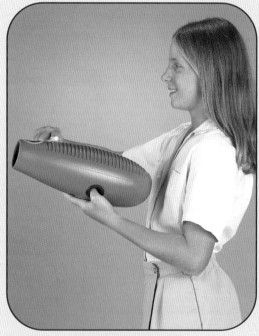

Play Position

- Draw the scraper across the grooves. Long and short scrapes can be played to match the note values indicated in the music.

- Scrape away from your body for long notes and toward your body for short notes.

- When the rhythms are fast, alternate directions on every note.

- A slow scrape produces a soft sound while a fast scrape is generally louder.

Creative Tools of Music

Units 16–18 are presented by your teacher

Allegro—fast tempo

Andante—slow (walking) tempo

Moderato—moderate or medium tempo

Rudiment

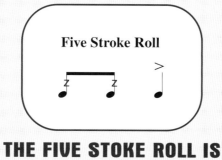

Five Stroke Roll

THE FIVE STOKE ROLL IS INTRODUCED IN 93 "OVER THERE"

89 *New Horizon Warm-Up*

90 *Finger Stretch*

91 *Marianne* CD :52

Folk Song, Jamaica

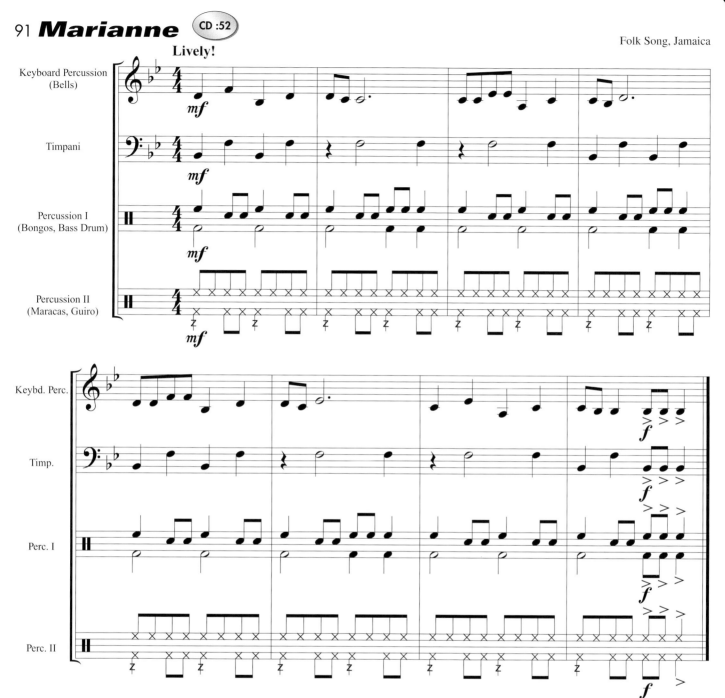

92 *Scooby-Doo, Where Are You?* CD :53

Words and Music by
DAVID MOOK and BEN RALEIGH

With energy!

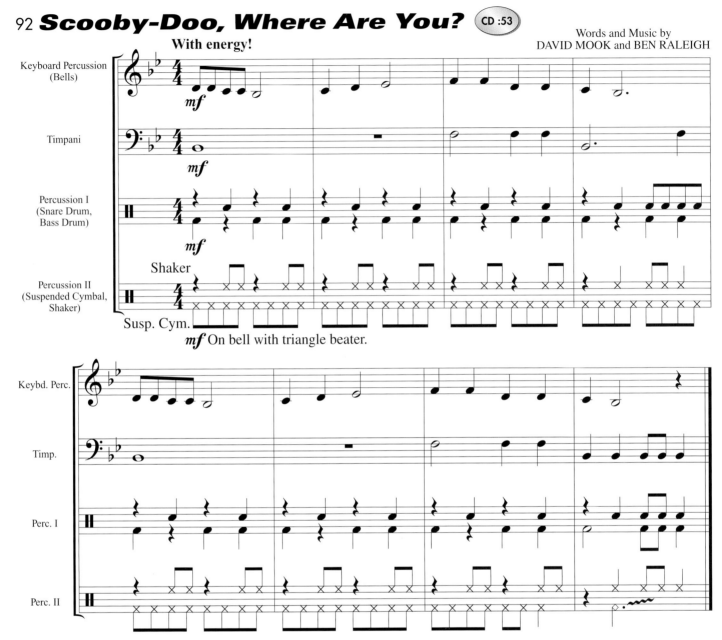

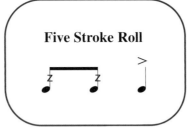

Five Stroke Roll

93 **Over There** CD :54

March

Words and Music by
GEORGE M. COHAN

Keyboard Percussion
(Bells)

Percussion I
(Snare Drum,
Bass Drum)

Cr. Cyms.

Percussion II
(Crash Cymbal,
Suspended Cymbal)

Susp. Cym.

Keybd. Perc.

Perc. I

Perc. II

Keybd. Perc.

Perc. I

Perc. II

94 *The Chicken Dance* CD :55
(a/k/a Dance Little Bird)

By TERRY RENDALL and WERNER THOMAS

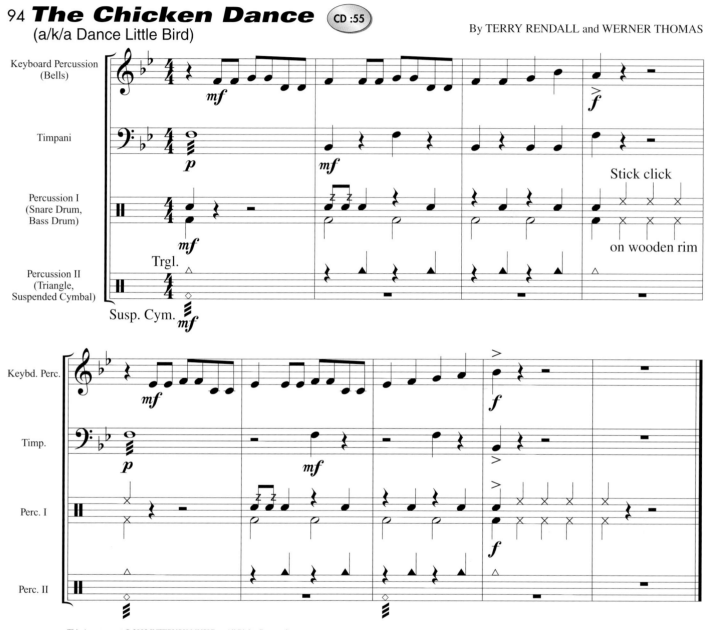

This Arrangement © 2003 INTERVOX MUSIC   All Rights Reserved

95 *Walking Waltz*

96 *Moderato March*

97 *Go, Go, Allegro!*

98 **Can Can** CD :56 CD :57 CD :58

Andante/Moderato/Allegro

JACQUES OFFENBACH, France

With S.D. stick

Band @ Home

 **LESSON 1**

1. Practice "Marianne" and "Scooby Doo, Where Are You?" with the accompaniment CD.

2. Perform "Marianne" and "Scooby Doo, Where Are You?" for a family member or friend. Ask them if they have heard these songs before and if so where.

3. Create a new sound by using the scrape technique on a variety of surfaces (gong, sauce pan, music stand, etc.)

 LESSON 2

1. Practice "Over There" and "The Chicken Dance."

2. Make up new appropriate motions to "The Chicken Dance" and teach them to someone in their family.

3. Continue to practice the Stroke Dexterity Exercises and the rudiments you have learned.

4. Practice your Five Stroke Rolls for clarity.

 **LESSON 3**

1 Practice "Can Can" at Moderato, Allegro, and Andante tempi.

2. Explain the different tempi to one of your family members and perform "Can Can" at those tempi.

3. Create an 8-measure rhythmic composition on the staff provided and then apply the tempo markings you have learned in this lesson—Moderato, Allegro, and Andante. Perform your composition using a selected note.

4. Continue to work on the Stroke Dexterity Exercises at different tempi. Practice all the rudiments you have learned so far.

9 *Creative Expression*

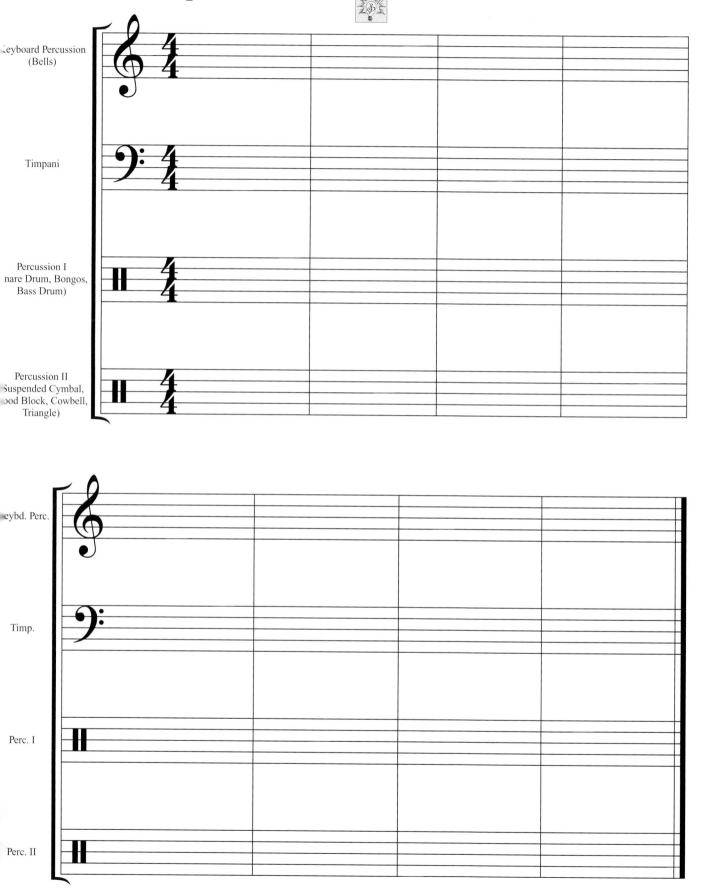

PORTRAIT

Aaron Copland
(1900-1990)

Aaron Copland composed musical works for ballets, orchestras, choirs, and the movies. He composed "Billy the Kid" and "Rodeo," music based on American folklore. He also composed "Lincoln Portrait," which was a tribute to President Abraham Lincoln. One of Copland's best-known works is "Fanfare for the Common Man."

Key of F

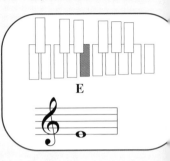

E

100 *Siren Warm-Up*

101 *Great Granddad*

Cowboy Song, U.S.A.

102 *Git Along Little Dogies*

Cowboy Song, U.S.A.

Go to the top of the next page.

Git Along Little Dogies, continued

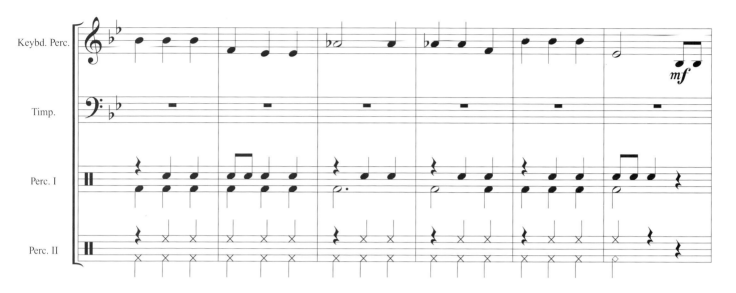

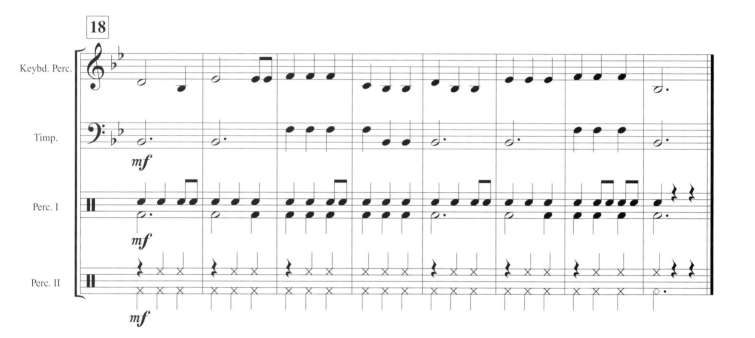

103 Goodbye Old Paint

Cowboy Song, U.S.A.

104 *Shaker Hymn*

Appalachian Folk Song, U.S.A.

Andante

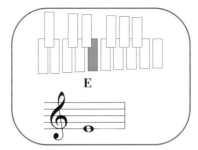

E

105 *Five Foot Two, Eyes of Blue*

Lyric by SAM LEWIS and JOE YOUNG
Music by RAY HENDERSON

106 **The Hey Song** CD :59

By MIKE LEANDER and GARY GLITTER

107 New for a Few

108 *Norwegian Mountain Dance*

Folk Song, Norway

109 **The Merry Go Round Broke Down** CD :60

Words and Music by
CLIFF FRIEND and DAVE FRANKLIN

Allegro

Keyboard Percussion (Bells or Xylophone)

Timpani

Percussion I (Snare Drum, Bongos, Bass Drum)

Play with brushes the first time, sticks the second time.

Wood Block

Percussion II (Suspended Cymbal, Wood Block)

Susp. Cym. (with S.D. stick) *f*

Keybd. Perc.

Timp.

(switch to sticks)

Perc. I

Perc. II

This Arrangement © 2003 WARNER BROS. INC.   All Rights Reserved

110 *Creative Expression* **Complete the Composition Worksheet #13.**

Rudiment Review Exercises

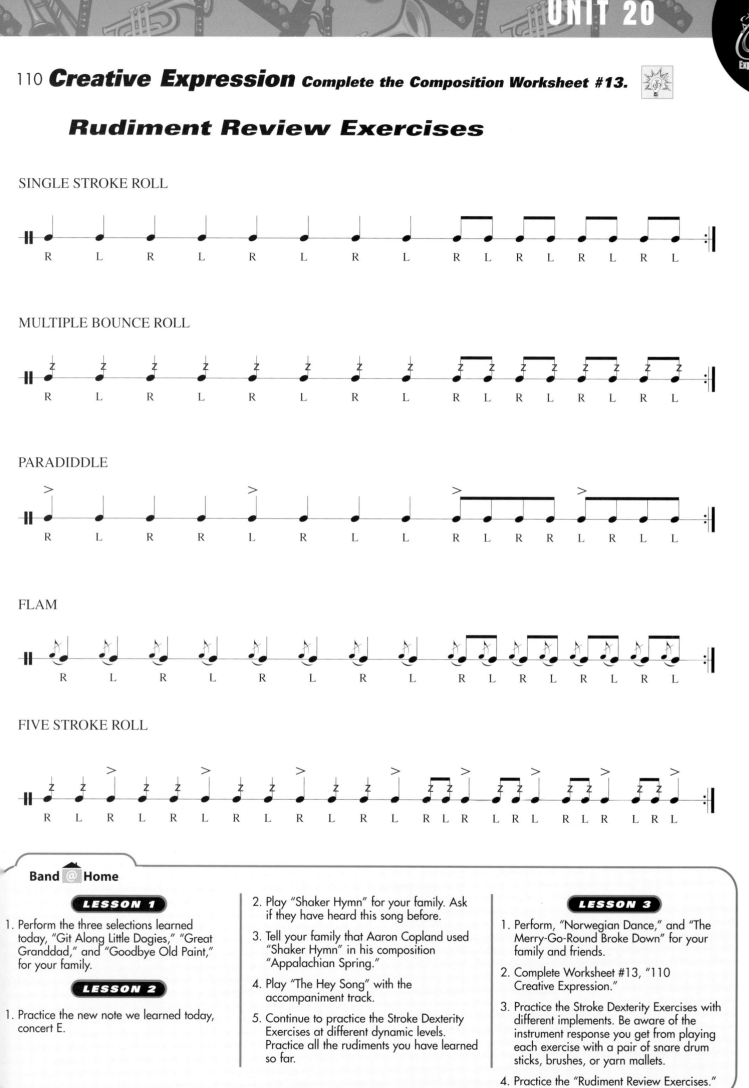

SINGLE STROKE ROLL

MULTIPLE BOUNCE ROLL

PARADIDDLE

FLAM

FIVE STROKE ROLL

Band @ Home

LESSON 1

1. Perform the three selections learned today, "Git Along Little Dogies," "Great Granddad," and "Goodbye Old Paint," for your family.

LESSON 2

1. Practice the new note we learned today, concert E.

2. Play "Shaker Hymn" for your family. Ask if they have heard this song before.

3. Tell your family that Aaron Copland used "Shaker Hymn" in his composition "Appalachian Spring."

4. Play "The Hey Song" with the accompaniment track.

5. Continue to practice the Stroke Dexterity Exercises at different dynamic levels. Practice all the rudiments you have learned so far.

LESSON 3

1. Perform, "Norwegian Dance," and "The Merry-Go-Round Broke Down" for your family and friends.

2. Complete Worksheet #13, "110 Creative Expression."

3. Practice the Stroke Dexterity Exercises with different implements. Be aware of the instrument response you get from playing each exercise with a pair of snare drum sticks, brushes, or yarn mallets.

4. Practice the "Rudiment Review Exercises."

Creative Tools of Music

𝄎 **Measure Repeat Sign—** a symbol that indicates to repeat the previous measure

2/4 **Time Signature—** 2 beats per measure Quarter note receives one beat

𝄾 **Eighth Rest—** receives one-half beat

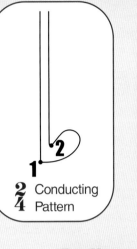

2/4 Conducting Pattern

Mariachi Cobre

Rudiment

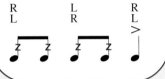

Nine Stroke Roll

R   L   R
L   R   L >

THE NINE STOKE ROLL IS INTRODUCED IN 113 "CUCU CUCU"

111 *Back to Home*

112 *Getting Even*

113 *Cucu Cucu*

Folk Song, Spain

116 *Eighth Rest Workout*

117 *Mi Caballo Blanco*

Folk Song, Chile

118 *Rest on the Beat*

119 *El Juego Chirimbolo* CD :62

Folk Song, Ecuador

120 *Relay Game*

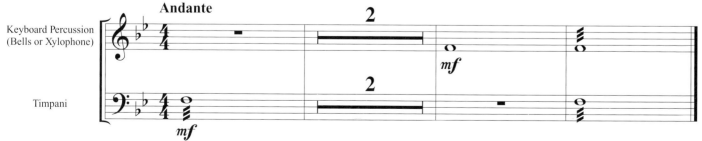

121 San Sereni

Folk Song, Latin America

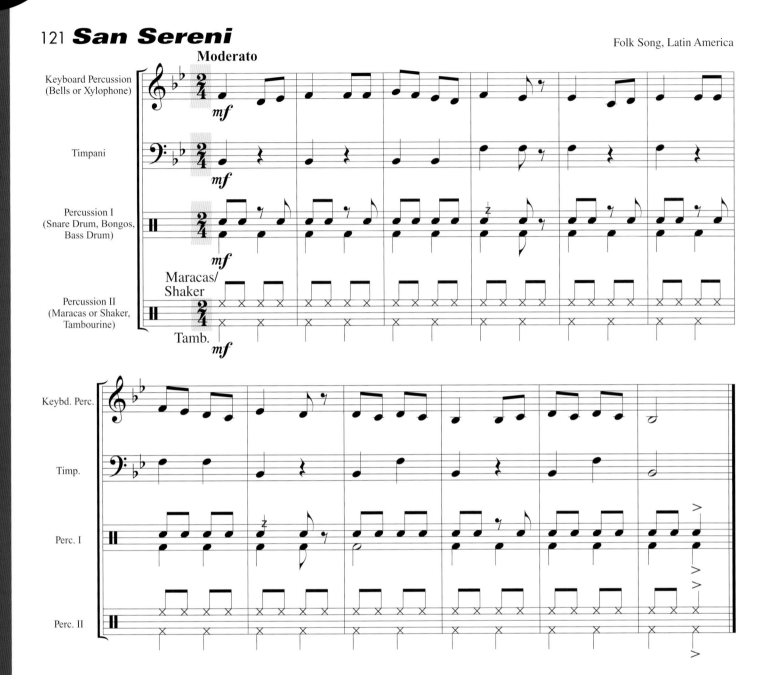

122 *La Cucaracha*

Folk Song, Mexico

123 *El Relicario* CD :63

Moderato

Folk Song, Mexico

Go to the top of the next page.

El Relicario, continued

124 *Creative Expression*

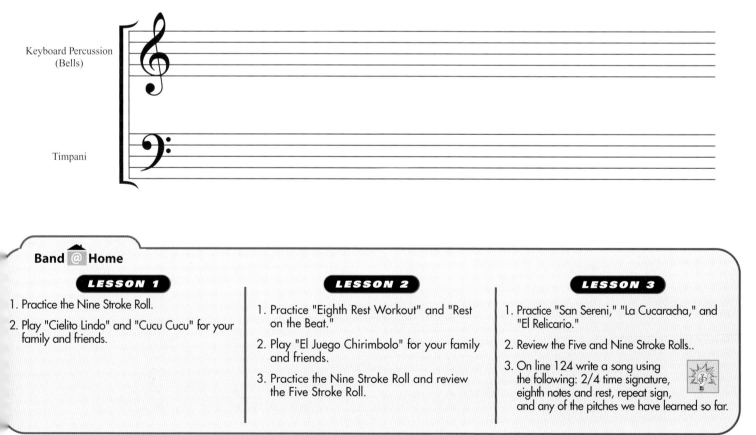

Band @ Home

LESSON 1

1. Practice the Nine Stroke Roll.

2. Play "Cielito Lindo" and "Cucu Cucu" for your family and friends.

LESSON 2

1. Practice "Eighth Rest Workout" and "Rest on the Beat."

2. Play "El Juego Chirimbolo" for your family and friends.

3. Practice the Nine Stroke Roll and review the Five Stroke Roll.

LESSON 3

1. Practice "San Sereni," "La Cucaracha," and "El Relicario."

2. Review the Five and Nine Stroke Rolls..

3. On line 124 write a song using the following: 2/4 time signature, eighth notes and rest, repeat sign, and any of the pitches we have learned so far.

Creative Tools of Music

Staccato—Firm grip, quick start, quick lift

Legato—Relaxed grip, smooth motion, natural rebound

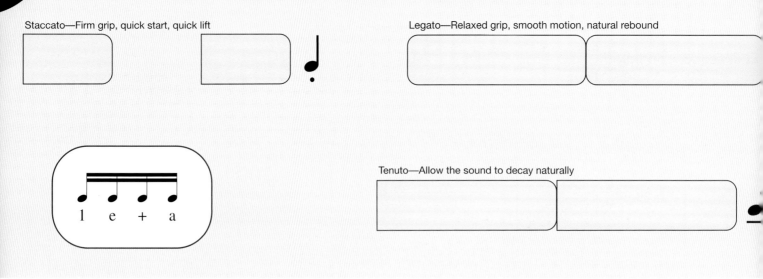

l   e   +   a

Tenuto—Allow the sound to decay naturally

125 *Theme From "The Surprise Symphony"* CD :64

FRANZ JOSEPH HAYDN, Austria

126 *Song of the Volga Boatmen*

Folk Song, Russia

127 *Paradiso* CD :65

By ROBERT W. SMITH

Gently

Keyboard Percussion (Bells)

mp legato

Percussion (Triangle, Suspended Cymbal)

Triangle

Susp. Cym. Scrape
legato

mp

Keybd. Perc.

Perc.

128 *Smooth Sailing*

Andante

Keyboard Percussion (Bells)

mf legato

Timpani

mf legato

Percussion I (Snare Drum, Bongos, Bass Drum)

mf

Triangle

Percussion II (Triangle, Suspended Cymbal)

mf

Susp. Cym. (with S.D. stick)

Keybd. Perc.

Timp.

Perc. I

Perc. II

129 *Dance of the Reed Flutes*

PETER ILYICH TCHAIKOVSKY, Russia

Moderato

130 The Long and Short of It

131 Sea Chanty CD :66

Traditional Sea Chanty, England

Go to the top of the next page.

ea Chanty, continued

132 *Can Can*

JACQUES OFFENBACH, France

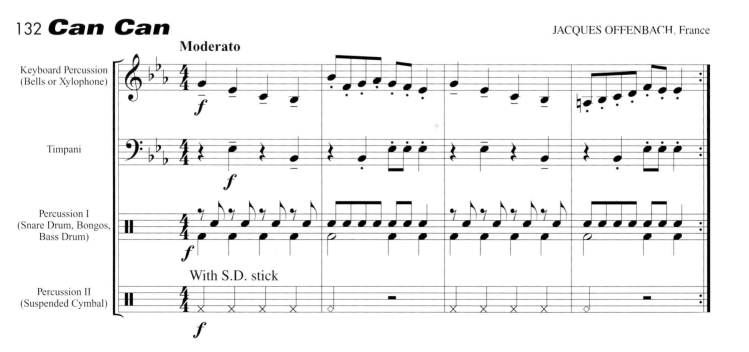

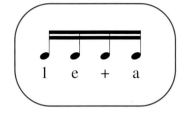

133 *Wipe Out* CD :67

By THE SURFARIS

Moderate rock

Go to the top of the next page.

Wipe Out, continued

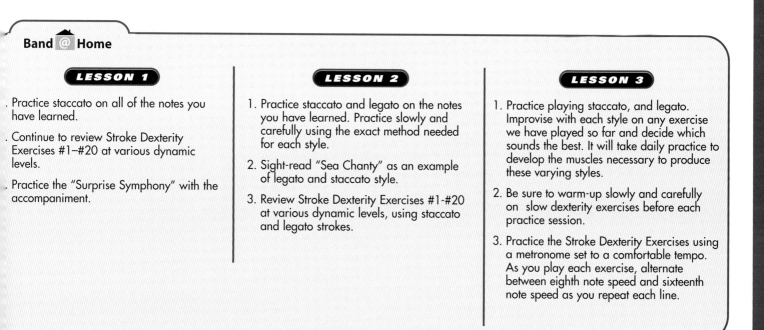

Band @ Home

LESSON 1

1. Practice staccato on all of the notes you have learned.

2. Continue to review Stroke Dexterity Exercises #1–#20 at various dynamic levels.

3. Practice the "Surprise Symphony" with the accompaniment.

LESSON 2

1. Practice staccato and legato on the notes you have learned. Practice slowly and carefully using the exact method needed for each style.

2. Sight-read "Sea Chanty" as an example of legato and staccato style.

3. Review Stroke Dexterity Exercises #1-#20 at various dynamic levels, using staccato and legato strokes.

LESSON 3

1. Practice playing staccato, and legato. Improvise with each style on any exercise we have played so far and decide which sounds the best. It will take daily practice to develop the muscles necessary to produce these varying styles.

2. Be sure to warm-up slowly and carefully on slow dexterity exercises before each practice session.

3. Practice the Stroke Dexterity Exercises using a metronome set to a comfortable tempo. As you play each exercise, alternate between eighth note speed and sixteenth note speed as you repeat each line.

The Art of Gong Playing

Setup Procedure

- The terms "gong" or "tam tam" are used interchangeably by composers to indicate an indefinite-pitched idiophone with a round shape and a flat surface. The gong should be hung freely from a sturdy stand. Use a large beater designed to play the gong, not a bass drum beater.

Rest Position

- The grip for the gong mallet is the same as that for the bass drum. Hold the stick with the right hand and use the left hand to muffle the gong from behind.

Ready Position

- A large gong may need to be "primed" to make it respond quickly with good tone. Prime the gong by softly tapping all over the surface with your hand or the gong beater prior to making a stroke.

Play Position

- Strike the surface of the gong just below the center to produce a full, deep tone.

- Lighter sounds may be produced by playing near the edge.

- Use your arm to throw the mallet directly toward the surface and quickly rebound it back to the starting position in one smooth motion. A long stroke uses the full motion of the arm that adds weight to the stroke to produce a loud volume.

- Use a shorter arm stroke to play softer.

- Play a series of quick strokes to produce a roll.

Dampen Position

- Use your left hand and leg to sto[p] the sound of the gong at the desired moment.

The Art of Bar Chimes Playing

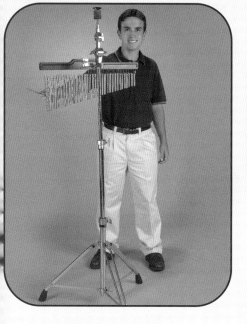

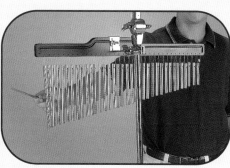

Ready Position

• Adjust the stand to bring the bar chimes to approximately chest level.

Setup Procedure

The bar chimes should be mounted to a cymbal stand so that the bracket is horizontal and the bars (or tubes) will hang freely.

The bar chimes should be set up in the proper location before rehearsal begins to avoid unnecessary noise.

Play Position

• Draw your fingers or a triangle beater across the metal tubes to set them in motion. Start with either the low end or high end as indicated in the music.

• Let the sound decay naturally.

• A slow scrape will produce a softer volume than a fast scrape.

The Art of Temple Blocks Playing

Ready Position

• The basic matched grip is the same as that for snare drum.

• A rubber mallet will give a full resonant sound and a snare drum stick will produce a lighter sound.

Setup Procedure

A stand and mounting bar are usually provided with a temple block set. The temple blocks should be flat and parallel to the floor.

Adjust the stand to bring the temple blocks to approximately waist level or slightly below.

The smallest temple block is usually placed to the player's right.

Play Position

• Using a wrist stroke similar to playing the snare drum, strike the block in the center over the open slit to produce the most resonant sound.

• Experiment with the playing area to find the exact "sweet spot" of each temple block.

Creative Tools of Music

Scenes of Daily Life in Korea, by Kim Junkeun

Crescendo—gradually get louder.

Decrescendo—gradually get softer.

Largo—very slow tempo

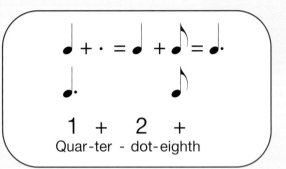

19th Century, ©Christie's Images Ltd. 1996

134 *Louder and Softer*

135 **Ouma**
CD :68
Mother Horse and Colt

Folk Song, Japan

136 *Sakura*
Cherry Blossoms

Folk Song, Japan

Susp. Cym.

137 *Kaeru No Uta (Duet)*

Folk Song, Japan

138 *Pentatonic Warm-Up*

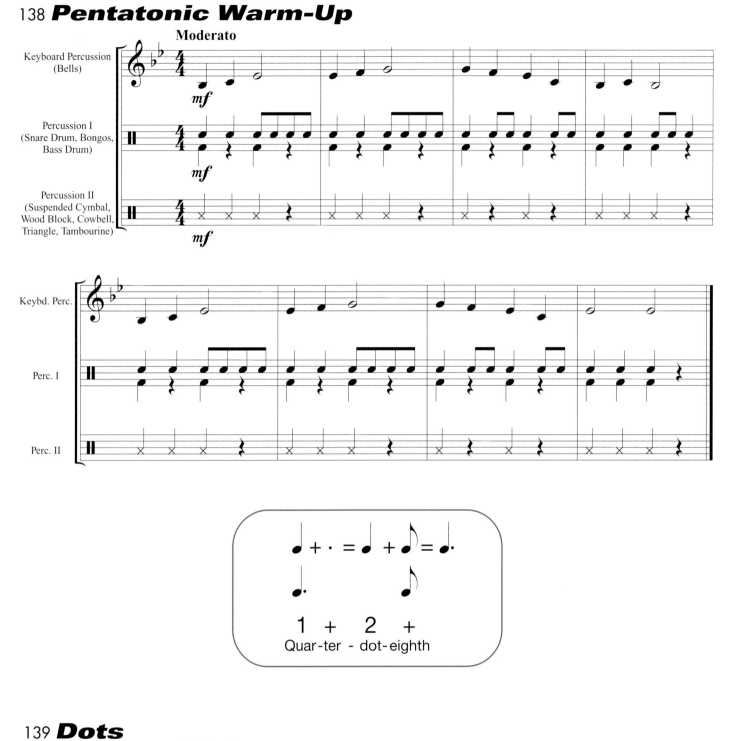

$$\bullet + \cdot = \bullet + \bullet = \bullet\cdot$$

1 + 2 +

Quar-ter - dot-eighth

139 *Dots*

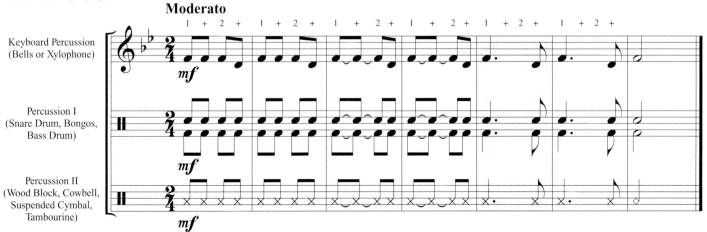

140 **Ha'kyo Jung** CD :69

Folk Song, Korea

141 **Hua Gu Ge**

Folk Song, China

142 *Arirang*

Folk Song, Korea

143 *Dotted Note Warm-Up*

144 Largo From "The New World Symphony"

ANTONÌN DVORÀK, Czechoslovakia

145 *Crescent Moon*

Folk Song, China

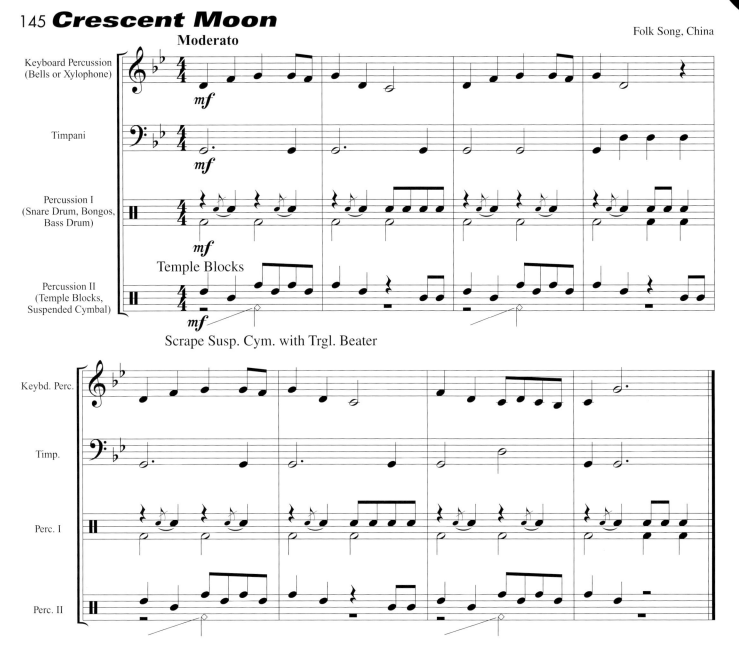

146 *Creative Expression* Compose a pentatonic melody and rhythm accompaniment on Worksheet #16.

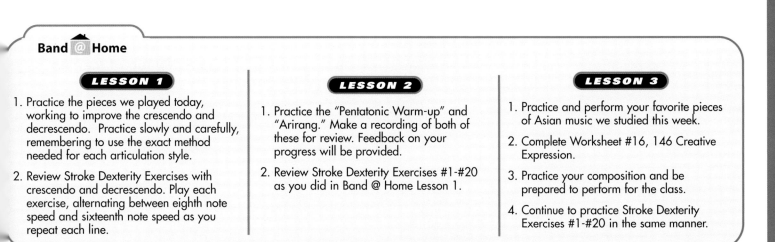

Band @ Home

LESSON 1

1. Practice the pieces we played today, working to improve the crescendo and decrescendo. Practice slowly and carefully, remembering to use the exact method needed for each articulation style.

2. Review Stroke Dexterity Exercises with crescendo and decrescendo. Play each exercise, alternating between eighth note speed and sixteenth note speed as you repeat each line.

LESSON 2

1. Practice the "Pentatonic Warm-up" and "Arirang." Make a recording of both of these for review. Feedback on your progress will be provided.

2. Review Stroke Dexterity Exercises #1-#20 as you did in Band @ Home Lesson 1.

LESSON 3

1. Practice and perform your favorite pieces of Asian music we studied this week.

2. Complete Worksheet #16, 146 Creative Expression.

3. Practice your composition and be prepared to perform for the class.

4. Continue to practice Stroke Dexterity Exercises #1-#20 in the same manner.

Please turn to pages 12–13, Unit 3 for the Art of Playing Marimb

Creative Tools of Music

Da Capo (D.C.)—return to the beginning

Fine—the end

Rudiment

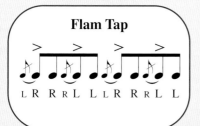

Flam Tap

L R R rL L L R R rL L

THE FLAM TAP IS INTRODUCED IN 149 GOLDEN GATE MARCH.

PORTRAIT

George Gershwin
(1898–1937)
George Gershwin's songs are some of the most lasting modern popular music written in the 20th Century. George Gershwin died when he was still fairly young. He is credited with being one of the first composers to merge jazz and classical music styles. One of his most famous works is the folk opera "Porgy and Bess."

147 *Low Tone Warm-Up*

Go to the top of the next page.

Low Tone Warm-Up, continued

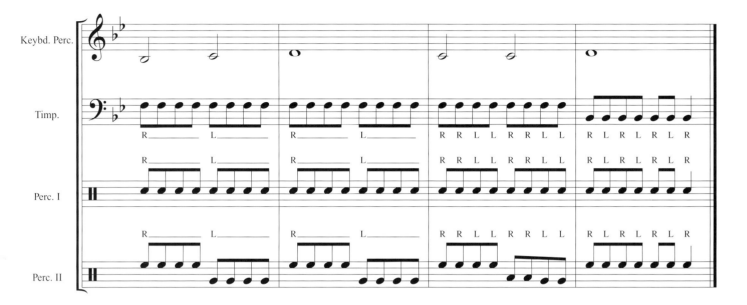

148 *Register Change Exercise*

149 *Golden Gate March*

150 *'S Wonderful* CD :70

Music and Lyrics by
GEORGE GERSHWIN and IRA GERSHWIN

Go to the top of the next page.

S Wonderful, continued

151 **Rhapsody in Blue™** CD :71

By GEORGE GERSHWIN

152 *The Donkey Song*

Traditional, U.S.A.

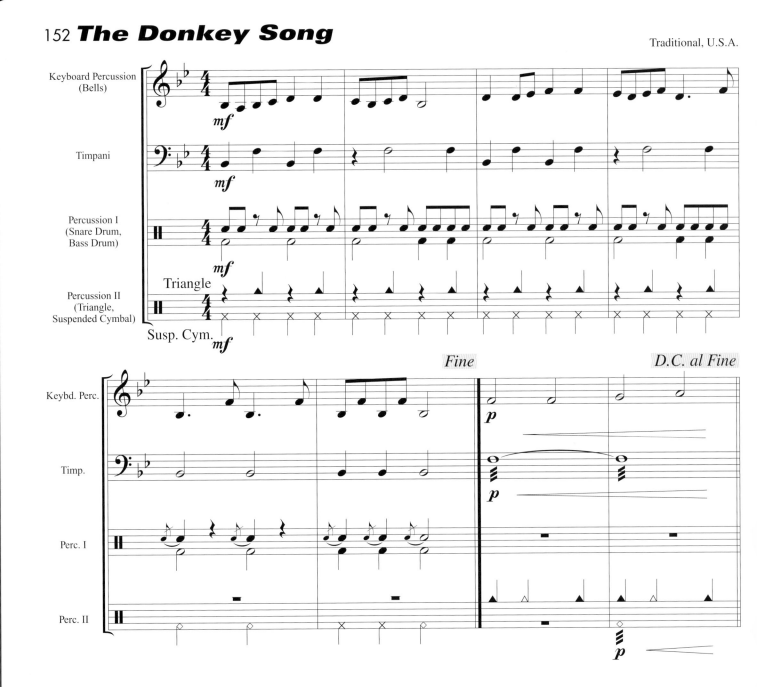

153 *Summertime* ⬭ CD :72

By GEORGE GERSHWIN, DuBOSE and
DOROTHY HEYWARD and IRA GERSHWIN

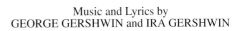

154 **I Got Rhythm** CD :73

Music and Lyrics by
GEORGE GERSHWIN and IRA GERSHWIN

Allegro

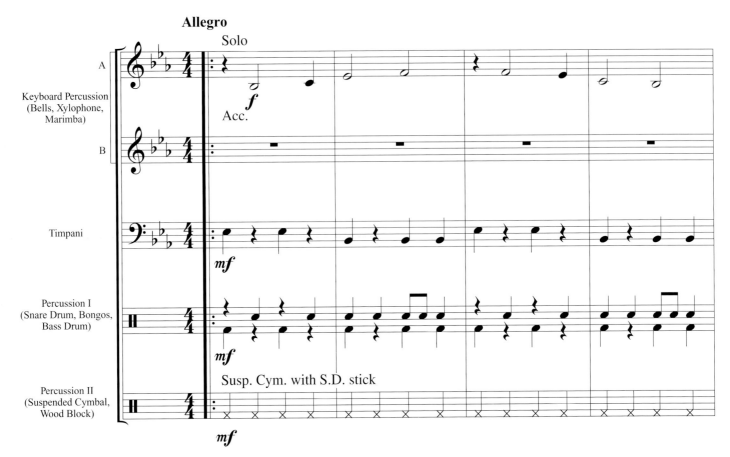

Go to the top of the next page.

I Got Rhythm, continued

I Got Rhythm - 2

D.C. al Fine

155 Creative Expression/Arrange and Notate
Arrange and notate on Worksheet #17.

Band @ Home

LESSON 1

1. Practice "Rhapsody in Blue" and "'S Wonderful."

2. Practice Flam Taps at a slow tempo, gradually increasing speed.

LESSON 2

1. Practice "Summertime" and "Donkey Song."

2. Review all the rudiments learned so far. Start by practicing each one slowly and gradually increase the tempo. Maintain control as you reach your top speed.

LESSON 3

1. Practice "Summertime" and "I Got Rhythm" with the accompaniment tracks.

2. Complete Worksheet #17, 155 Creative Expression.

3. Continue to review all the rudimetns you have learned so far. Maintain control as you practice each one slowly and gradually increase the tempo.

Rudiment Review Exercises

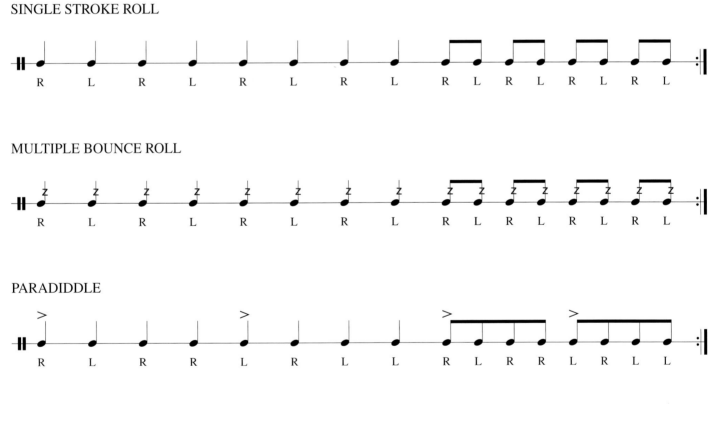

SINGLE STROKE ROLL

R L R L R L R L R L R L R L R L

MULTIPLE BOUNCE ROLL

R L R L R L R L R L R L R L R L

PARADIDDLE

R L R R L R L L R L R R L R L L

Rudiment "Breakdown"

60 seconds

Review these rudiments that you have learned:

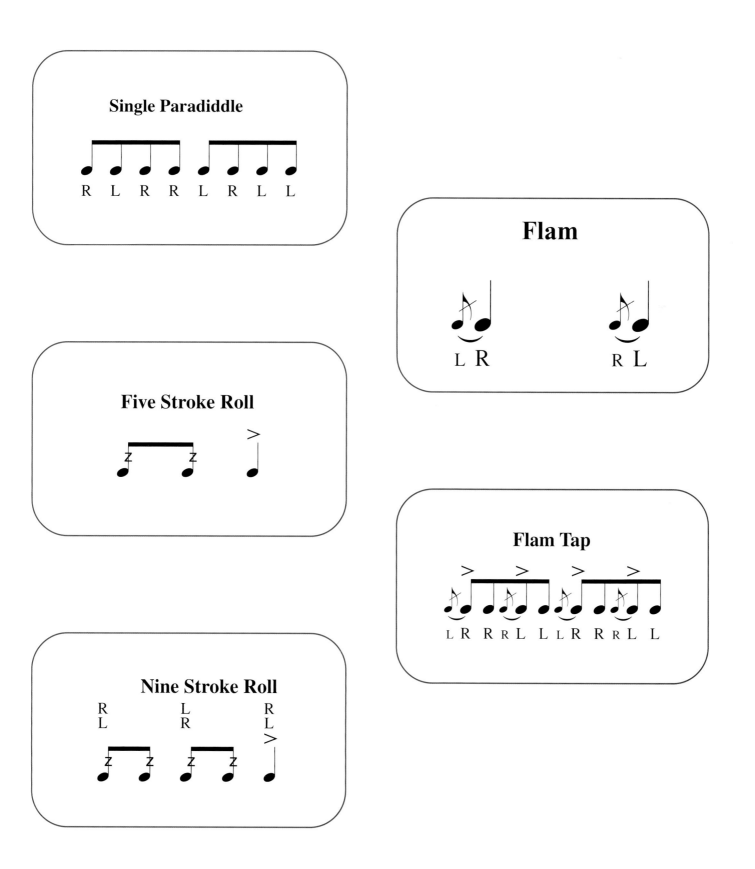

Single Paradiddle

R L R R L R L L

Flam

L R   R L

Five Stroke Roll

Flam Tap

L R R r L L L R R r L L

Nine Stroke Roll

R   L   R
L   R   L

Creative Tools of Music

Drum Circle—an interactive group of people gathered in a circle to play music on percussion instruments; a facilitator who directs the group in rhythm activities and improvised patterns usually leads a drum circle

Ritardando (Rit.)—gradually slow down

Syncopation—rhythm with the emphasis or stress on a weak beat or weak portion of a beat

Down	Up	(Down)	Up
1	+	(2)	+

Celebration, by Charles Searles (b. 1937)

©Smithsonian American Art Museum, Washington, D.C., Art Resource, N.Y.

156 *You're a Grand Old Flag*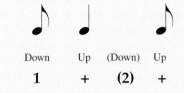

GEORGE M. COHAN, U.S.A.

Go to the top of the next page.

You're a Grand Old Flag, continued

157 *Hill and Gully* CD :75

Caribbean

158 *Cheki, Morena*

Folk Song, Puerto Rico

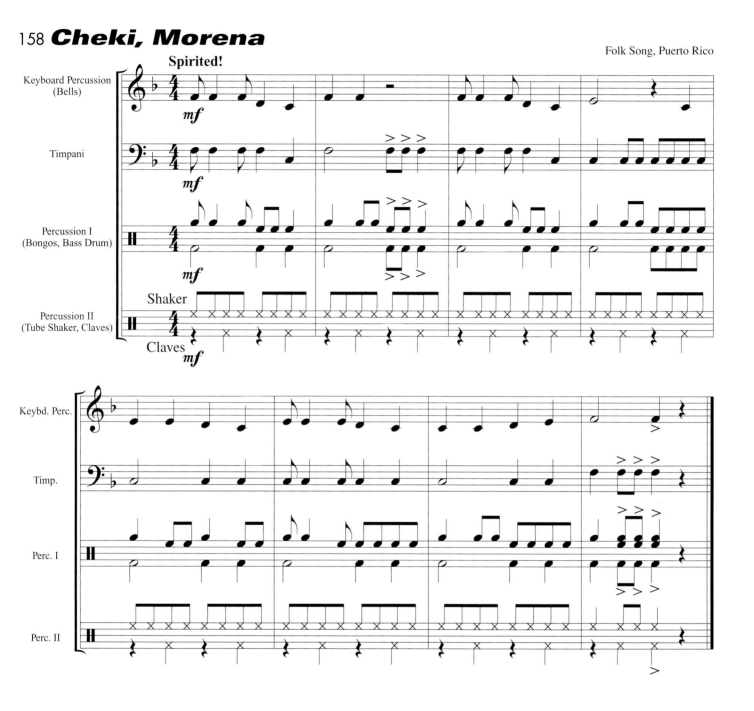

159 African Warm-Up

Marilli

160 *Che Che Koolay* CD :76

161 *The Rooster's Call*

Folk Song, Liberia

162 *Green Sally Up*

Folk Song, U.S.A.

163 *Hello Lungile* CD :77

Folk Song, South Africa

164 *Lil' Liza Jane*

Words and Music by
COUNTESS ADA DELACHAU, U.S.A.

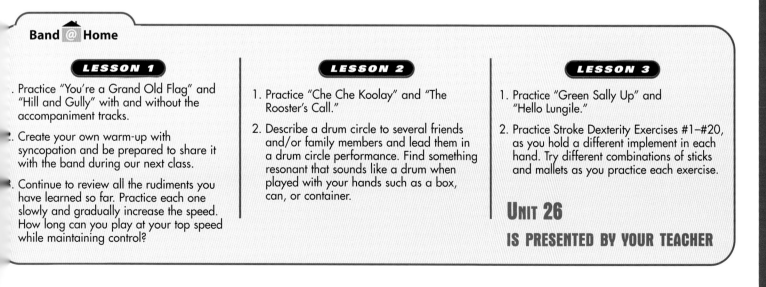

Snare Drum and Suspended Cymbal: Right hand plays with a Snare Drum stick, left hand plays with a brush.
Slide the brush over the surface when 𝄾 is notated.

Band @ Home

LESSON 1

1. Practice "You're a Grand Old Flag" and "Hill and Gully" with and without the accompaniment tracks.

2. Create your own warm-up with syncopation and be prepared to share it with the band during our next class.

3. Continue to review all the rudiments you have learned so far. Practice each one slowly and gradually increase the speed. How long can you play at your top speed while maintaining control?

LESSON 2

1. Practice "Che Che Koolay" and "The Rooster's Call."

2. Describe a drum circle to several friends and/or family members and lead them in a drum circle performance. Find something resonant that sounds like a drum when played with your hands such as a box, can, or container.

LESSON 3

1. Practice "Green Sally Up" and "Hello Lungile."

2. Practice Stroke Dexterity Exercises #1–#20, as you hold a different implement in each hand. Try different combinations of sticks and mallets as you practice each exercise.

UNIT 26

IS PRESENTED BY YOUR TEACHER

UNIT 26 IS PRESENTED BY YOUR TEACHER

Please turn to pages 12-13, Unit 3 for the Art of Playing Vibraphon

The Art of Playing Hi-Hat

Setup Procedure

1. Stand or sit on a stool so that your left foot rests comfortably on the footboard.

2. The hi-hat is played with the foot alone or the top cymbal is struck with a snare drum stick as it coordinates with the motion of the foot.

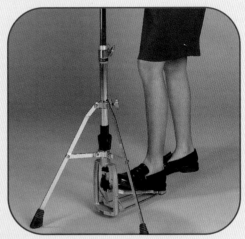

Ready Position

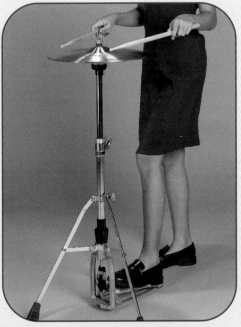

Play Position

- Place your left foot flat on the footboard so that the high-hat remains open.

- Make a rocking motion with your foot. The toe presses the footboard do and the heel lifts to close the cymbals. The heel moves down and the toe lifts to open the cymbals.

- The cymbals should produce a tight "chick" sound when they are broug together.

- Keep the entire foot relaxed throughout the stroke as the natural spring the high-hat stand should help keep the cymbals open.

- The hi-hat cymbals may be struck when the cymbals are fully opened, fu closed, or partially closed when the cymbals are lightly making contact.

Creative Tools of Music

Jazz—music rooted in improvisation and characterized by syncopated rhythms

𝄋 Dal Segno (D.S.)—repeat from the sign

Improvisation—the process of spontaneously creating a new melody

Swing—a style of jazz music characterized by the "lengthening" of the eighth notes that are on the beat

PORTRAIT

Edward Kennedy "Duke" Ellington
(1899-1974)

Duke Ellington is remembered as one of the greatest jazz artists and important composers of the Twentieth Century. He wrote thousands of compositions, which included jazz music, sacred music for the church, show music, and music for movies. Mr. Ellington composed jazz classics such as "It Don't Mean a Thing (If it Ain't Got That Swing)" and "Satin Doll." He was also a brilliant conductor, arranger, pianist, and bandleader.

165 *Gentle Warm-Up*

166 *Chorale*

167 *Angel Band*

African-American Folk Song, U.S.A.

168 Duke's Place CD :78
(a/k/a C Jam Blues)

Music by DUKE ELLINGTON
Lyrics by RUTH ROBERTS, BILL KATZ and ROBERT THIELE

169 *New Note Warm-Up*

170 **Wade in the Water** CD :79

Spiritual

African-American Spiritual, U.S.A.

171 *It Don't Mean a Thing (If It Ain't Got That Swing)*

Words and Music by
DUKE ELLINGTON and IRVING MILLS

172 *Satin Doll*   CD :80

Music by DUKE ELLINGTON

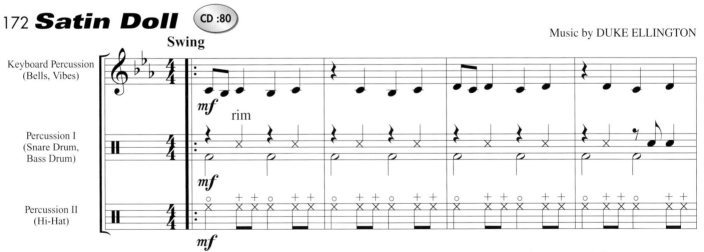

Go to the top of the next page.

atin Doll, continued

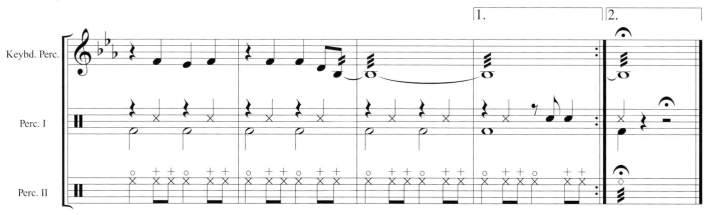

My Warm-Up Exercises

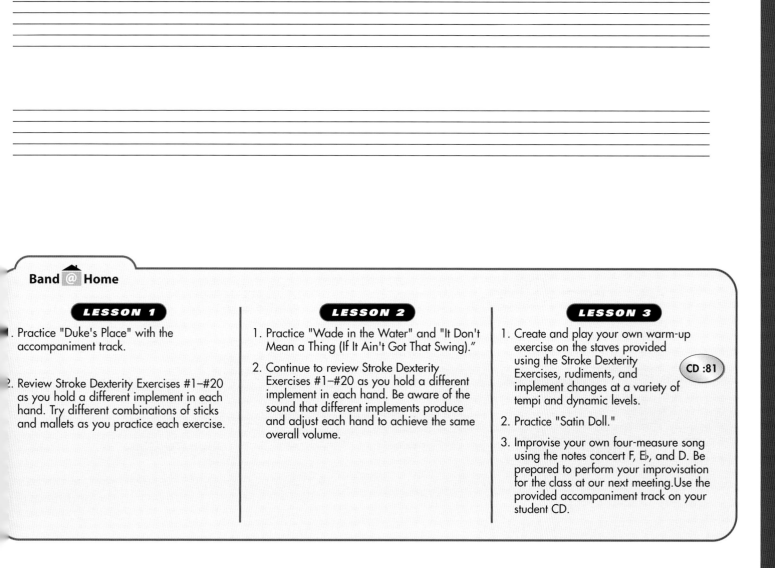

Band @ Home

LESSON 1

1. Practice "Duke's Place" with the accompaniment track.

2. Review Stroke Dexterity Exercises #1–#20 as you hold a different implement in each hand. Try different combinations of sticks and mallets as you practice each exercise.

LESSON 2

1. Practice "Wade in the Water" and "It Don't Mean a Thing (If It Ain't Got That Swing)."

2. Continue to review Stroke Dexterity Exercises #1–#20 as you hold a different implement in each hand. Be aware of the sound that different implements produce and adjust each hand to achieve the same overall volume.

LESSON 3

1. Create and play your own warm-up exercise on the staves provided using the Stroke Dexterity Exercises, rudiments, and implement changes at a variety of tempi and dynamic levels.

CD :81

2. Practice "Satin Doll."

3. Improvise your own four-measure song using the notes concert F, E♭, and D. Be prepared to perform your improvisation for the class at our next meeting. Use the provided accompaniment track on your student CD.

The Art of Playing Claves

Setup Procedure

- Place the claves on a padded surface for easy access.

Ready Position

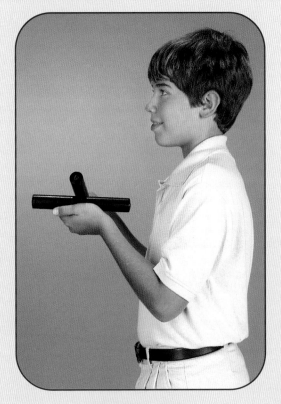

Play Position

- Hold the clave at eye level so that you can easily watch it, the conductor, and the music.

- Hold the other clave near the end.

- Hold one clave gently with the fingertips of one hand to form a trough underneath. The clave should rest lightly in your hand so that it makes the most resonant sound possible.

- Using a wrist stroke similar to playing the snare drum, strike the clave in the middle with the other clave to produce a piercing, resonant tone.

- Experiment with the playing area to find the exact "sweet spot" of the claves.

Creative Tools of Music

Half Step—the distance between two adjacent notes

Interval—the distance between two pitches

Scale—a stepwise progression used in melodies and harmonies

Whole step—a musical distance that equals two half steps

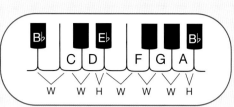

Rudiment

Drag

L L R   R R L

THE DRAG IS INTRODUCED IN 177 "CHESTER."

	W	W	H	W	W	W	H
	1	2	3	4	5	6	7	8
Concert Key	B♭	C	D	E♭	F	G	A	B♭
C Instruments	B♭	C	D	E♭	F	G	A	B♭
B♭ Instruments	C	D	E	F	G	A	B	C
E♭ Instruments	G	A	B	C	D	E	F♯	G
F Instruments	F	G	A	B♭	C	D	E	F

1 + a   1 e +
R R L   R L R

173 *There Are Many Flags in Many Lands*

Traditional, U.S.A.

174 *Oranges and Lemons*

Folk Song, England

UNIT 28

175 **Tinga Layo** CD :82

Folk Song, Jamaica

165

176 Concert B♭ Scale Warm-Up

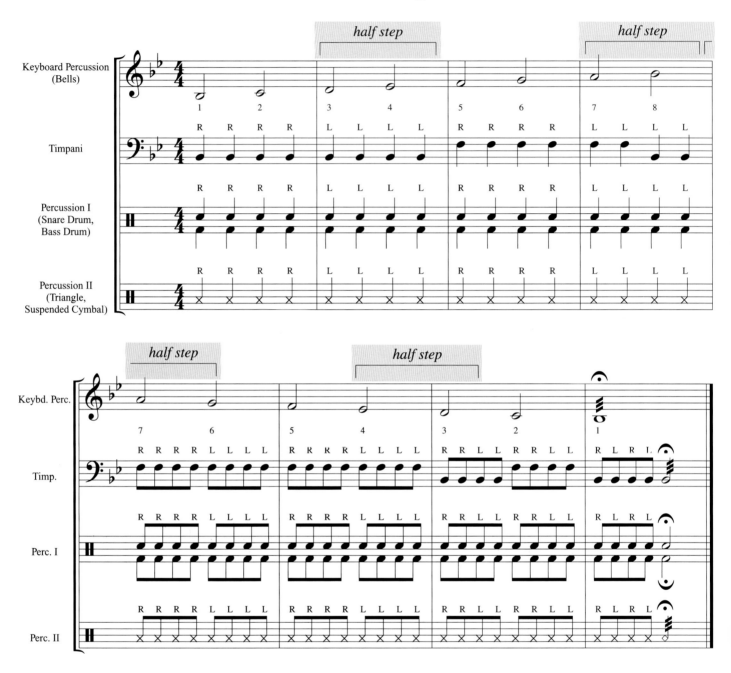

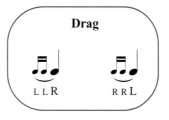

Drag

L L R   R R L

177 *Chester*

WILLIAM BILLINGS, U.S.A.

178 *Peep Squirrel* CD :83

Folk Song, Africa

179 *Hao Peng You*

Folk Song, China

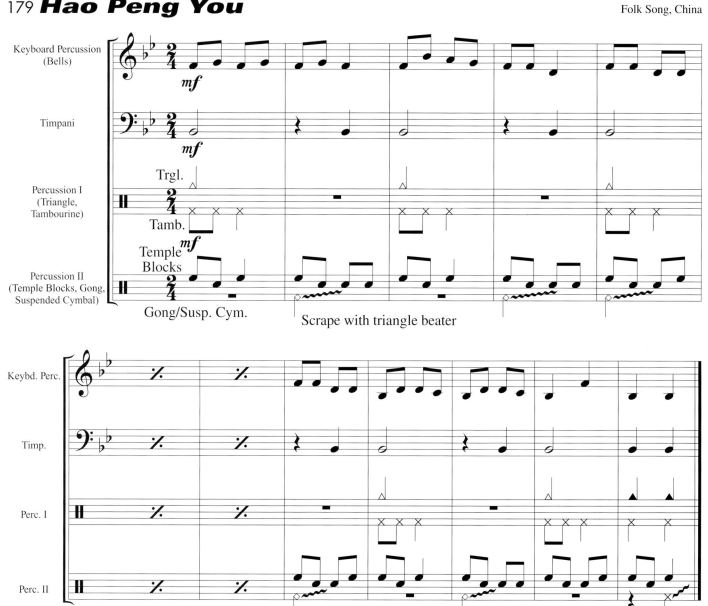

180 *Kookabura*

By MARION SINCLAIR

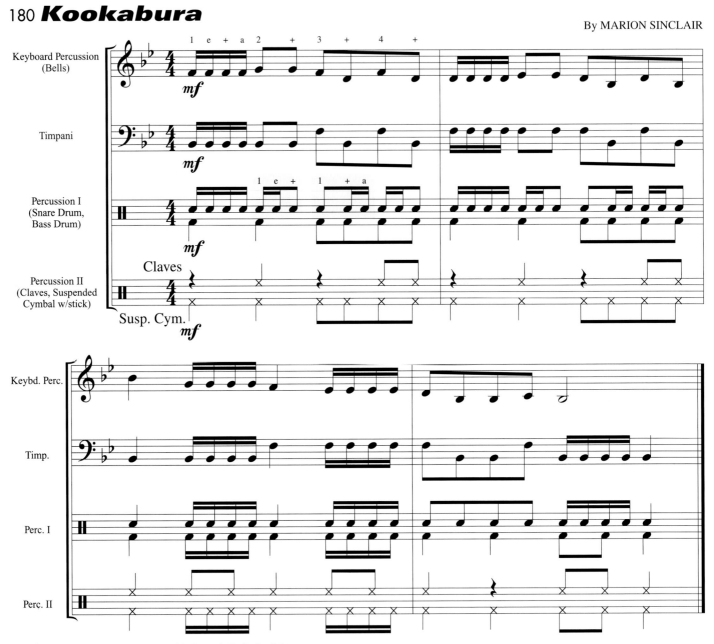

181 **Ciranda** CD :84

Folk Song, Brazil

182 *Over the Rainbow*

Music by HAROLD ARLEN
Lyric by E.Y. HARBURG

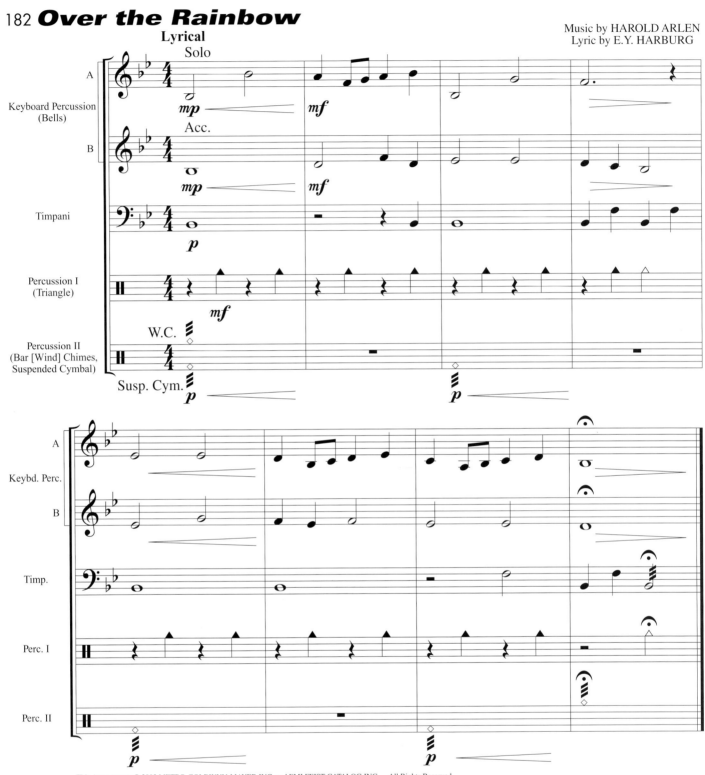

Keyboard Percussion

183 Creative Expression

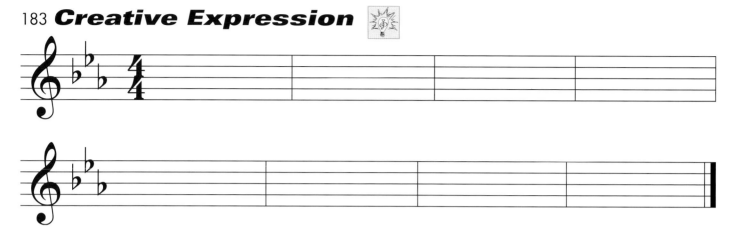

Timpani

183 Creative Expression

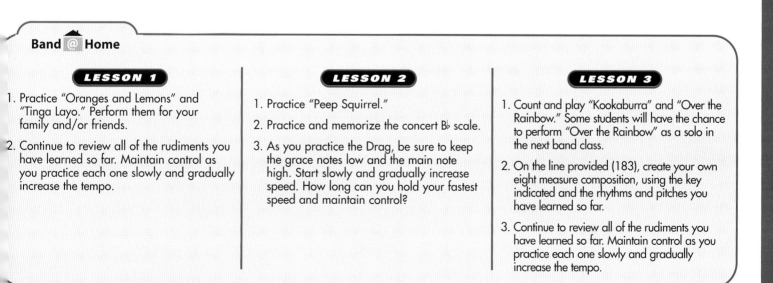

Band @ Home

LESSON 1

1. Practice "Oranges and Lemons" and "Tinga Layo." Perform them for your family and/or friends.

2. Continue to review all of the rudiments you have learned so far. Maintain control as you practice each one slowly and gradually increase the tempo.

LESSON 2

1. Practice "Peep Squirrel."

2. Practice and memorize the concert Bb scale.

3. As you practice the Drag, be sure to keep the grace notes low and the main note high. Start slowly and gradually increase speed. How long can you hold your fastest speed and maintain control?

LESSON 3

1. Count and play "Kookaburra" and "Over the Rainbow." Some students will have the chance to perform "Over the Rainbow" as a solo in the next band class.

2. On the line provided (183), create your own eight measure composition, using the key indicated and the rhythms and pitches you have learned so far.

3. Continue to review all of the rudiments you have learned so far. Maintain control as you practice each one slowly and gradually increase the tempo.

The Art of Playing Concert Toms

Setup Procedure

- Concert toms are traditionally played with snare drum sticks or hard felt mallets.

- The drums should be flat and parallel to the floor. Adjust the stand to bring the top head to approximately waist level or slightly below.

- The high drum may be placed on either the player's right or left to best accommodate the music.

Tuning

- The tom heads should be tensioned until a natural rebound feels comfortable with the stick.

- The drums should be tuned about a third apart in pitch.

- The proper playing area is slightly off center on each drum.

Care and Maintenance

- Use a cloth to keep the entire drum clean and free of fingerprints, dust, and dirt.

- Keep all objects off of the drum head, it's not a table.

- The average life of a drum head is one year. Replace worn or damaged heads immediately.

- A small dab of lithium grease or lubrication should be applied to the tension rods when the heads are replaced.

Ready Position

- The basic matched grip is the same as that for snare drum.

Play Position

- Use the same ready position as that for snare drum.

Play Position

- Use the same full stroke as that for snare drum.

The Art of Playing Finger Cymbals

Setup Procedure

- A single finger cymbal can be suspended from a triangle clip and struck with a triangle beater to accommodate quick instrument changes or when playing multiple instruments.

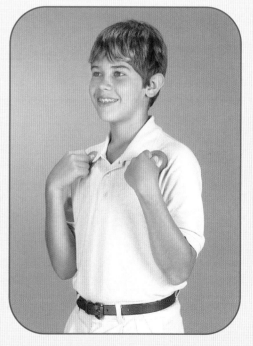

Ready Position

Hold the pair of finger cymbals by the straps, at eye level, with the edges perpendicular to each other.

Play Position

- Strike the edge of one cymbal against the edge of the other.

Dampen Position

- Dampen against the body after the stroke is made to control the amount of sustain.

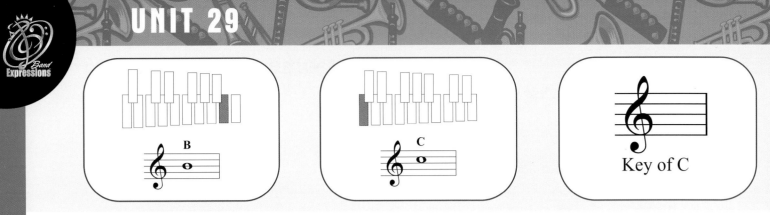

Key of C

184 *Lip Slurs*

Creative Tools of Music

Multiple Percussion—Playing two or more percussion instruments at the same time.

135 *On the High "C's"* CD :86

186 *Wabash Cannonball*

Traditional, U.S.A.

187 **Matchmaker, Matchmaker** CD :85

Lyrics by SHELDON HARNICK
Music by JERRY BOCK

UNIT 29

188 *Sleeping Beauty*

PETER ILYICH TCHAIKOVSKY, Russia

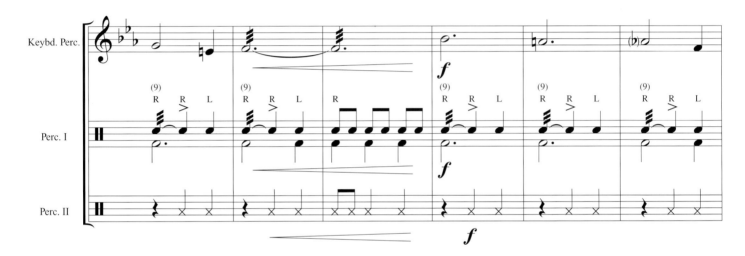

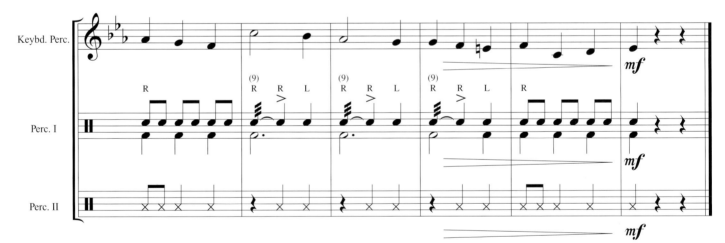

189 *"B" Your Best*

5-stroke roll

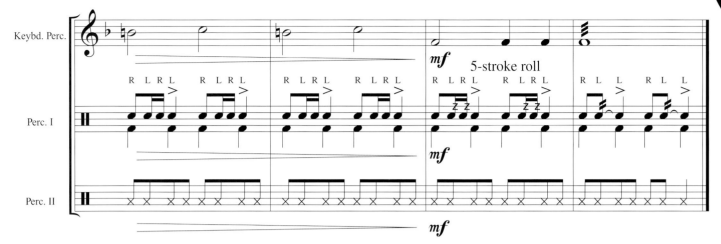

190 Theme From Ice Castles (Through the Eyes of Love)

Music by MARVIN HAMLISCH
Lyrics by CAROLE BAYER SAGER

191 Concert C Major Scale

Keyboard Percussion (Bells)

192 Santa Lucia

Folk Song, Italy

Moderato

Keyboard Percussion (Bells)

Timpani

Percussion I (Snare Drum, Bongos, Bass Drum)

Percussion II (Finger Cymbals)

193 Doo Wah Diddy Diddy

CD :87

Words and Music by
JEFF BARRY and ELLIE GREENWICH

Moderato

Keyboard Percussion (Bells)

Timpani

One player on Susp. Cym. and S.D./Bongos

Percussion I (Suspended Cymbal, Snare Drum, Bongos, Bass Drum)

(One player)

Percussion II (Cowbell, Concert Tom)

This Arrangement © 2003 Trio Music Co., Inc. and Universal - Songs of PolyGram International, Inc.   All Rights Reserved

194 **The Hey Song** CD :88

By MIKE LEANDER and GARY GLITTER

Rudiment Review Exercises

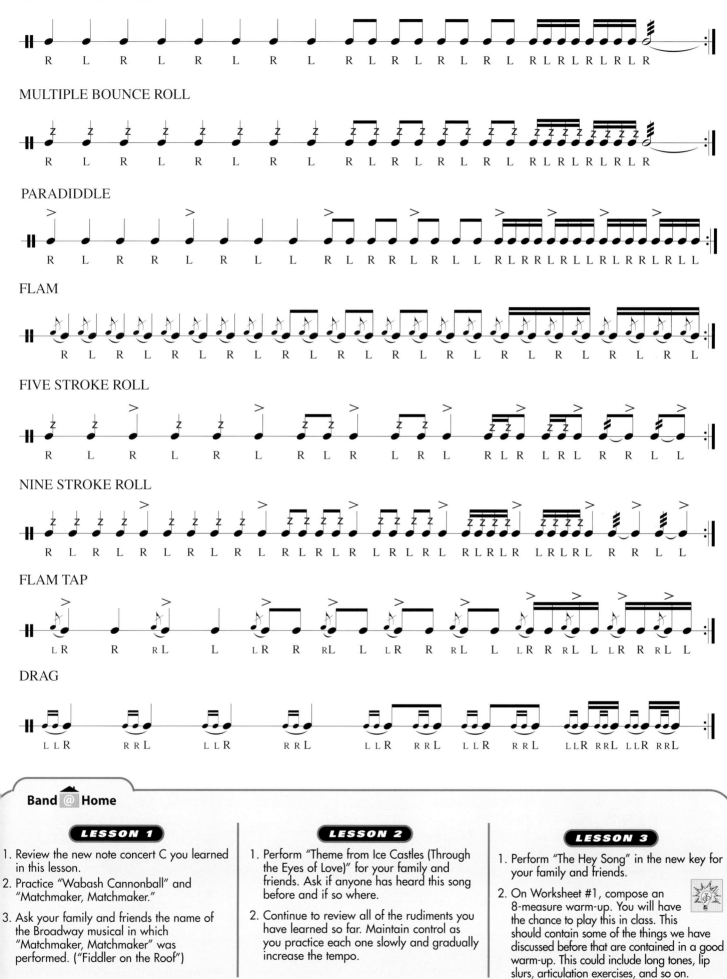

SINGLE STROKE ROLL

MULTIPLE BOUNCE ROLL

PARADIDDLE

FLAM

FIVE STROKE ROLL

NINE STROKE ROLL

FLAM TAP

DRAG

Band @ Home

LESSON 1

1. Review the new note concert C you learned in this lesson.
2. Practice "Wabash Cannonball" and "Matchmaker, Matchmaker."
3. Ask your family and friends the name of the Broadway musical in which "Matchmaker, Matchmaker" was performed. ("Fiddler on the Roof")

LESSON 2

1. Perform "Theme from Ice Castles (Through the Eyes of Love)" for your family and friends. Ask if anyone has heard this song before and if so where.
2. Continue to review all of the rudiments you have learned so far. Maintain control as you practice each one slowly and gradually increase the tempo.

LESSON 3

1. Perform "The Hey Song" in the new key for your family and friends.
2. On Worksheet #1, compose an 8-measure warm-up. You will have the chance to play this in class. This should contain some of the things we have discussed before that are contained in a good warm-up. This could include long tones, lip slurs, articulation exercises, and so on.

The Art of Playing Hand Cymbals

Rest Position

Setup Procedure

- Hand cymbals should be placed on a padded surface to make their pickup and replacement as silent as possible.

Care and Maintenance

- Use a dry cloth or a mild solution of warm water and dish soap to keep the cymbal clean and free of fingerprints and stick marks.

- Use a professional cymbal cleaner for deep cleaning.

Grip

- Place the strap across the palm of the hand. Curl the fingers around the strap and make a fist, placing t thumb against the top of the bell.

- A small leather cymbal pad may b used to cushion the fingers.

Ready Position

- Place the cymbal in your strong hand slightly above the other cymbal at approximately chest level. Hold the cymbals apart at a slight angle to each other.

Dampen Position

- Dampen the cymbals against the chest or shoulders to stop the sound.

Play Position

- For a full crash, move the cymbal in your strong hand in a downward motion toward the other cymbal.

- The upper cymbal will strike the lower cymbal at the bottom edge, as it moves upward to meet the upper cymbal. All the edges will meet during the follow through motion of the crash. The sound created is similar to a Flam.

- Both cymbals must be in motion, in opposite directions, to produce the fullest tone.

- The louder the volume, the further apart you must start the cymbals in motion.

Play Position

- To play a soft crash, place the cymbals parallel, 1" to 3" apart, an gently bring them together so that all edges touch at the same time.

- Let the cymbals move apart naturally as part of the crash mot

- Do not redirect the cymbals to fac the front after the crash.

John Philip Sousa
(1854–1932)

Sometimes known as the "March King," John Philip Sousa wrote some of the most famous and recognizable marches in the world. Sousa was born in 1854 and he started studying music at the age of 6. When he was 13 years old his father enlisted Sousa in the Marines after he tried to run away from home to play in a circus band. In 1880, Sousa was appointed conductor of the United States Marine Band in Washington DC, which is known as "The President's Own." He later organized the Sousa Band and traveled the country presenting concerts with this organization. Throughout his illustrious career, Sousa wrote over 130 marches. In 1987, his "Stars and Stripes Forever" became the official march of the United States of America.

195 *More Lip Slurs*

196 Caissons Go Rolling Along

CD :89

EDMUND L. GRUBER

(With S.D. stick)

197 *Marines Hymn*

Traditional, U.S.A.

198 *Anchors Aweigh*

CD :90

Words and Music by
Capt. ALFRED H. MILES, U.S.N. (Ret.) and CHAS. A. ZIMMERMANN

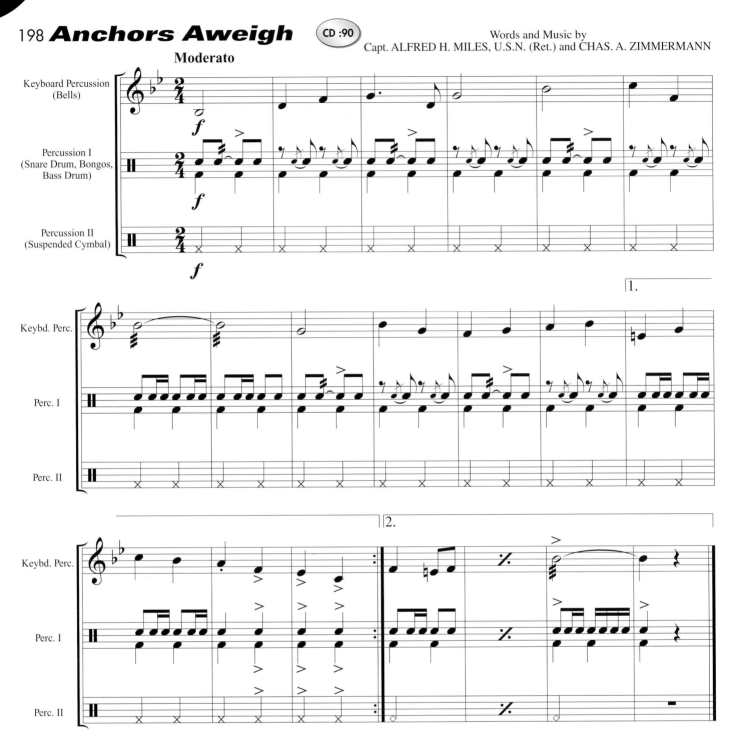

199 *El Capitan*

JOHN PHILIP SOUSA, U.S.A.

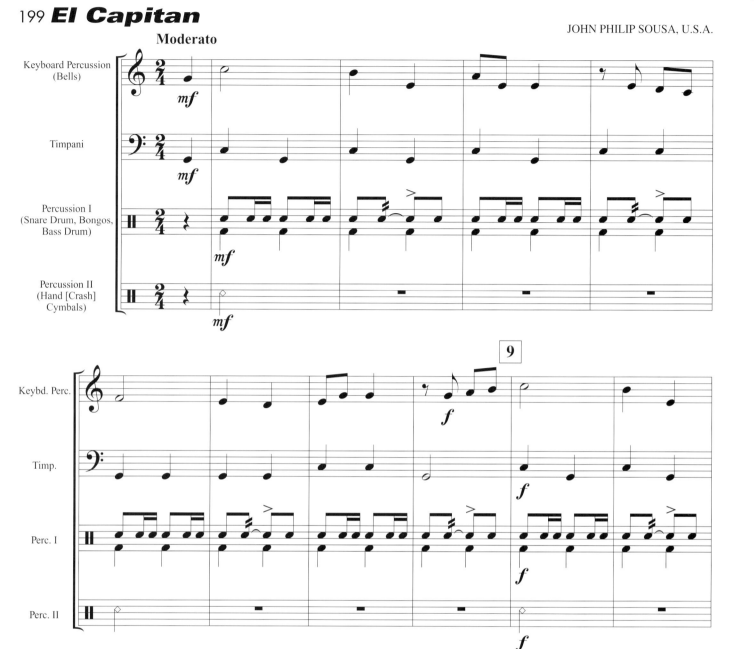

200 *The Thunderer*

JOHN PHILIP SOUSA, U.S.A.

ROLL BASE CHART

Roll Type	Notated as	Performed as a Multiple Bounce Roll
Five Stroke Roll		R L R / L R L
Nine Stroke Roll		R L R L R / L R L R L
Seventeen Stroke Roll		R L R L R L R L R / L R L R L R L R L

201 *Blow Away the Morning Dew*

Folk Song, England

202 The Yellow Rose of Texas CD :91

Folk Song, U.S.A.

203 Na Na Hey Hey CD :92
(Kiss Him Goodbye)

Words and Music by
GARY DE CARLO, DALE FRASHUER and PAUL LEKA

Band @ Home

LESSON 1

1. Practice the Double Stroke Roll by alternating hands. Begin slowly, gradually playing faster until a smooth, even, sustained sound is achieved. How long can you play at your top speed while maintaining control?

2. Practice "Caissons Go Rolling Along," "The Marines Hymn," and "Anchors Aweigh."

3. Ask your family members if they can identify which branch of the U.S. Armed Services these marches represent.

LESSON 2

1. Remember to start your practice session with the proper warm-up.

2. Teach your family and friends about the composer John Philip Sousa.

3. Play "El Capitan" and "The Thunderer" for your family and friends.

4. Continue to practice the Double Stroke Roll by alternating hands.

LESSON 3

1. Practice "Blow Away the Morning Dew," "The Yellow Rose of Texas," and "Na Na Hey Hey (Kiss Him Goodbye)."

2. As you practice these three pieces, remember to play with the best sound possible.

3. Practice rolls of different lengths as both Multiple Bounce Rolls and Double Stroke Rolls.

The Art of Playing Kick Drum and Chimes

Setup Procedure

- Stand behind the kick drum with your feet comfortably spread apart.

- Sitting on a stool will help the taller player to better position the leg properly and to work the pedal more efficiently.

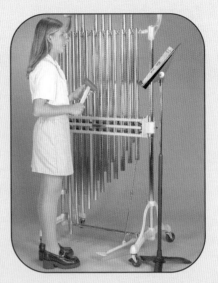

Setup Procedure

- Place the music stand close to the side of the chimes and use peripheral vision to see the chimes while watching the music and the conductor.

Ready Position

- Place your right foot flat on the bass drum pedal. Stay relaxed so that the beater remains off the head.

Play Position

- Make a quick downward stroke with your toe to sound the kick drum. Relax the foot to allow the beater to naturally spring from the head.

- Keep the entire foot relaxed and in contact with the pedal throughout the stroke

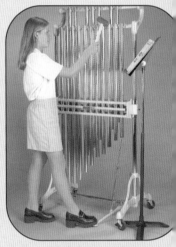

Ready Position

- Depress the pedal mechanism on the chimes to let the tubes resonate. Use a mallet or hammer specially designed for concert chimes.

Play Position

- Make a quick stroke to strike the side of the ca on the tube.

Johann Sebastian Bach
(1685–1750)

Johann Sebastian Bach was one of the most important composers in European history. He was a church musician all of his life and people today still regularly sing and play his music in church. He did not play the piano until he was an old man, so most of his keyboard music was composed for the organ or clavichord, a very popular keyboard instrument during the Baroque era. The Baroque era style included much ornamentation that was added to clothing, furniture, and architecture. Baroque music also was very ornamented.

204 **Down and Up**

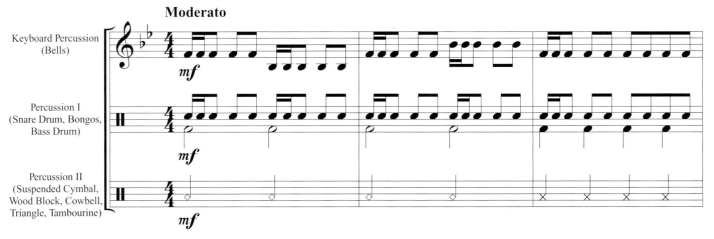

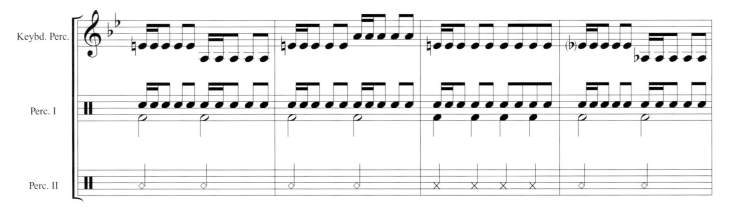

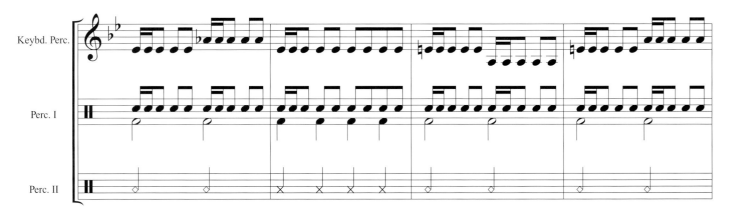

205 **Manhattan Beach** CD :93

JOHN PHILIP SOUSA, U.S.A.
Arranged by MICHAEL STORY

Manhattan Beach - 2

21

29

Quickly turn the page and continue on the top of page 200.

Manhattan Beach - 3

206 **Arirang** CD :94

Folk Song, Korea
Arranged by MICHAEL STORY

Moderato

Quickly turn the page and continue on the top of page 202.

Arirang - 2

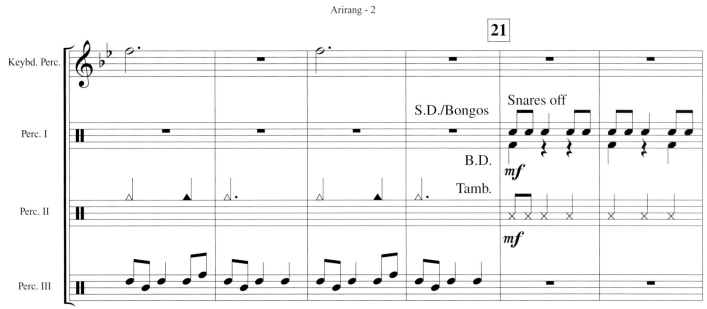

Arirang - 3

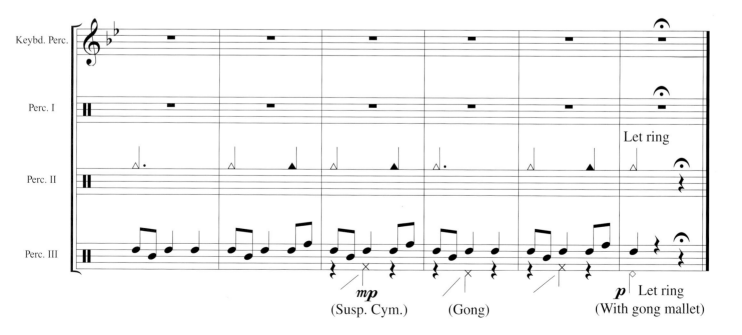

207 **Expressions in Blue** CD :95

ROBERT W. SMITH

Expressions in Blue - 2

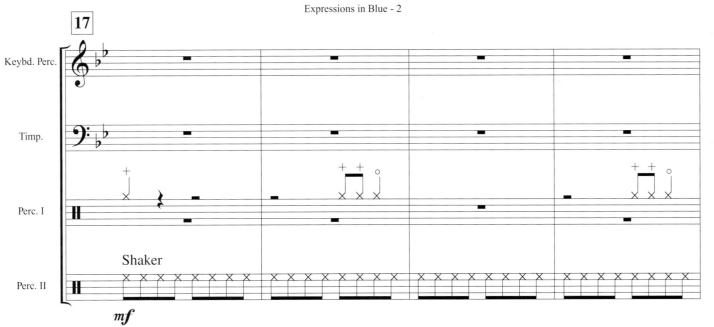

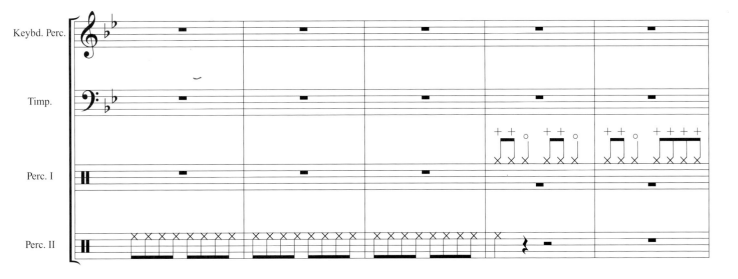

Quickly turn the page and continue on the top of page 206.

Expressions in Blue - 3

Expressions in Blue - 4

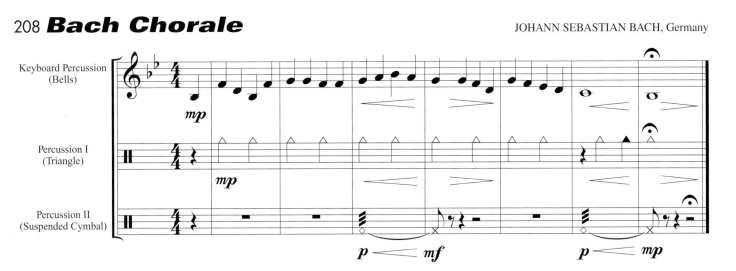

208 **Bach Chorale**

JOHANN SEBASTIAN BACH, Germany

209 **Let Freedom Ring** CD :96

Traditional
Arranged by ROBERT W. SMITH

Let Freedom Ring - 2

Quickly turn the page and continue on the top of page 210.

Let Freedom Ring - 3

Let Freedom Ring - 4

30 *"America, the Beautiful"*
Flowing

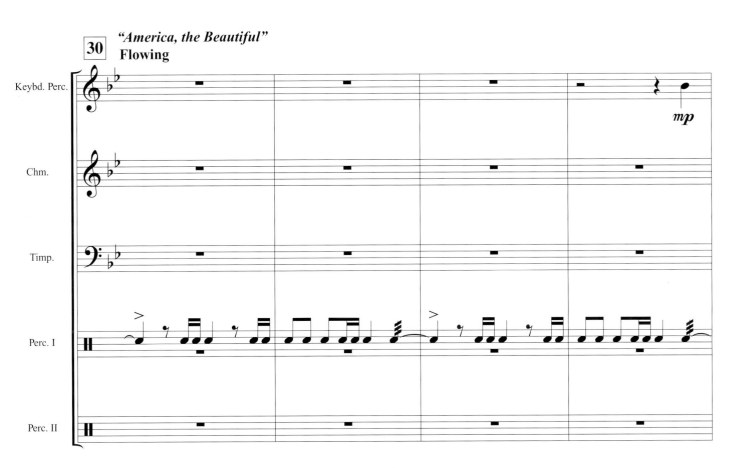

Quickly turn the page and continue on the top of page 212.

Let Freedom Ring - 5

Let Freedom Ring - 6

Eine Kleine Nachtmusik

WOLFGANG AMADEUS MOZART, Austria

Over the Rainbow (Solo)

Music by HAROLD ARLEN
Lyric by E.Y. HARBURG

Timpani Solo

2 for 24

JAMES CAMPBELL

Snare Drum Solo

March Navarre

JAMES CAMPBELL

Music for the Royal Fireworks

GEORGE FRIDERIC HANDEL, Germany/England
Arranged by SANDRA DACKOW

Band @ Home

LESSON 1 & **LESSON 2**

1. Be sure to warm-up slowly and carefully before each practice session. Include a review of Stroke Dexterity Exercises with a different implement in each hand.

2. Review all of our concert pieces we have played so far. Practice the kick drum part to "Expressions in Blue" by using a drum set or tap your foot on the floor.

3. Remember to isolate the more difficult passages, playing them slowly before gradually increasing the speed.

4. Make a recording of your performance of each piece and turn it in at our next lesson. Write down what you discovered from critically listening to yourself play. Your teacher will review your recording and provide feedback for improvement.

5. Practice the solos on page 210 "Over the Rainbow" and "Eine Kleine Nachtmusik," and perform them for family and friends.

6. Practice the timpani solo "2 for 24" and the snare drum solo "March Navarre" on page 211.

UNITS 33–36
ARE PRESENTED BY YOUR TEACHER

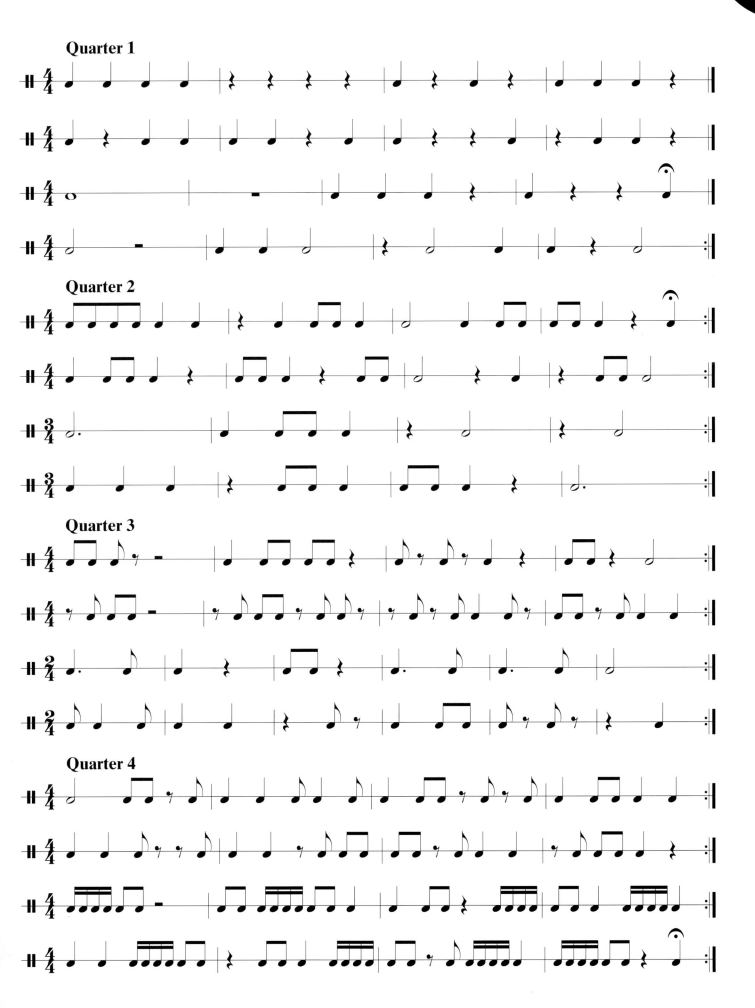

Treasury of Scales: Concert B♭

Treasury of Scales: Concert E♭

Treasury of Scales: Concert F

Treasury of Scales: Concert C

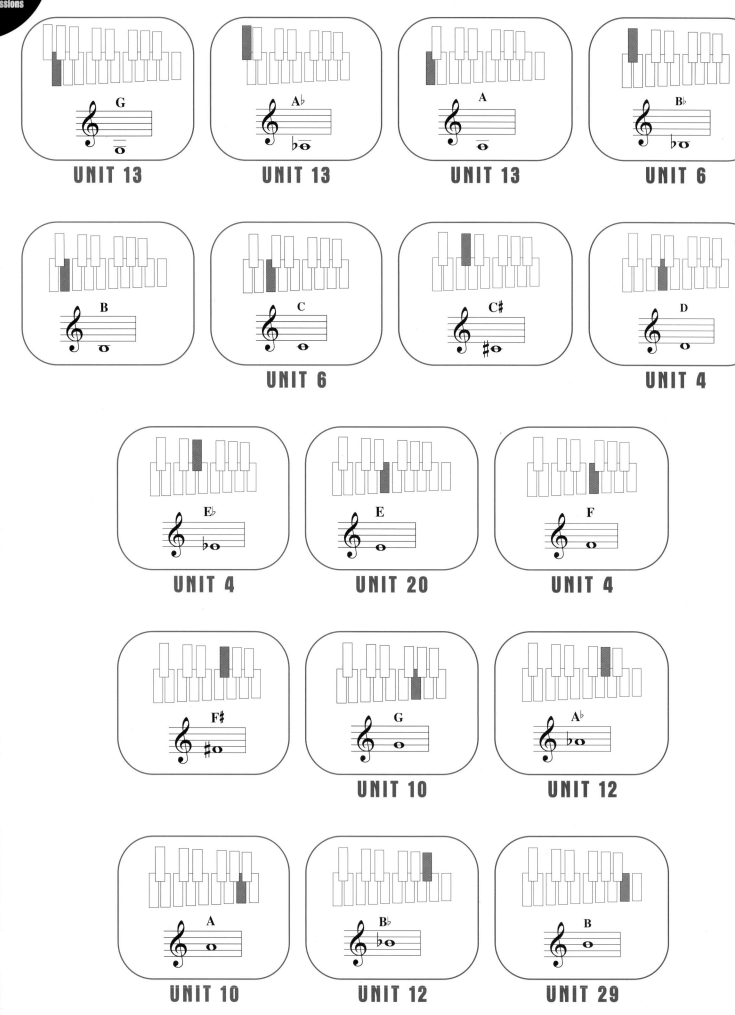

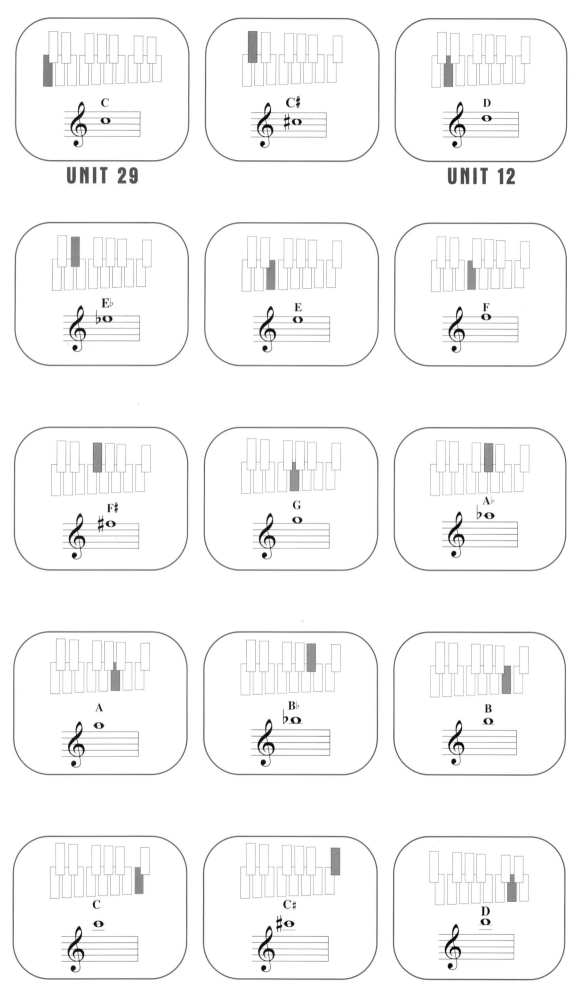

UNIT 29

UNIT 12

Marimba, Vibraphone, Xylophone Only

The Percussive Arts Society International Drum Rudiments

I. ROLL RUDIMENTS

A. Single Stroke Roll Rudiments

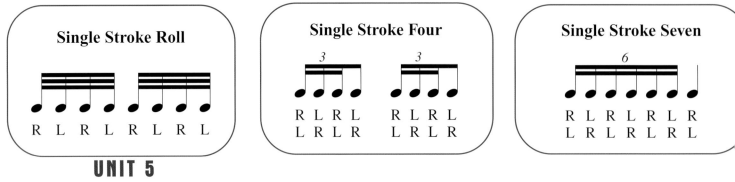

Single Stroke Roll	Single Stroke Four	Single Stroke Seven
R L R L R L R L	R L R L / L R L R R L R L / L R L R	R L R L R L R / L R L R L R L
UNIT 5		

B. Multiple Bounce Roll Rudiments

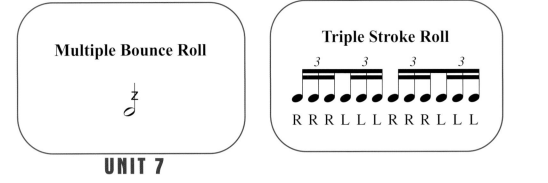

Multiple Bounce Roll	Triple Stroke Roll
	R R R L L L R R R L L L
UNIT 7	

C. Double Stroke Open Roll Rudiments

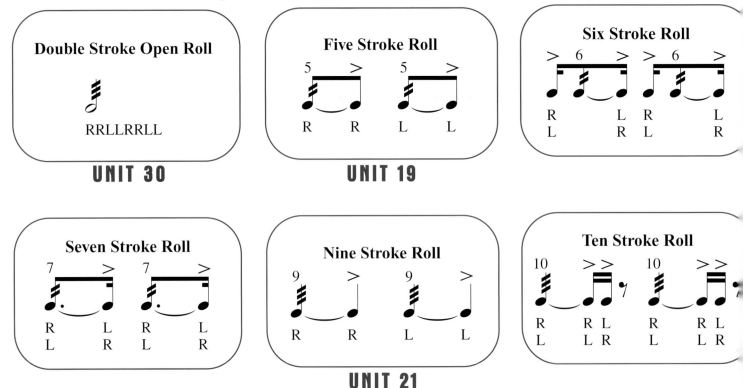

Double Stroke Open Roll	Five Stroke Roll	Six Stroke Roll
RRLLRRLL	R R L L	R L L R R L L R
UNIT 30	**UNIT 19**	

Seven Stroke Roll	Nine Stroke Roll	Ten Stroke Roll
R L L R R L L R	R R L L	R L R L / L R R L L R
	UNIT 21	

C. Double Stroke Open Roll Rudiments, continued on top of next page

C. Double Stroke Open Roll Rudiments, continued.

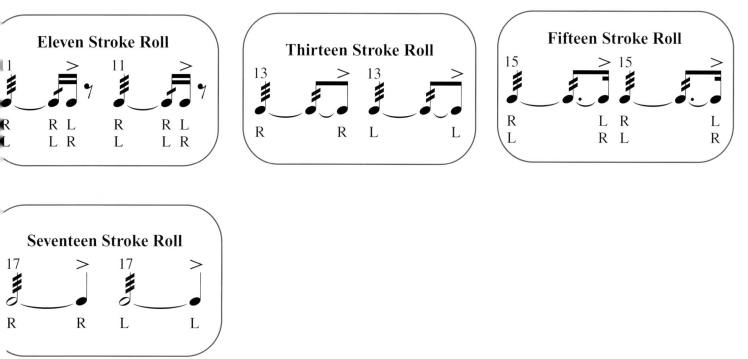

Eleven Stroke Roll

11 > 11 >

R R L R R L
L L R L L R

Thirteen Stroke Roll

13 > 13 >

R R L L

Fifteen Stroke Roll

15 > 15 >

R L R L
L R L R

Seventeen Stroke Roll

17 > 17 >

R R L L

UNIT 30

I. DIDDLE RUDIMENTS

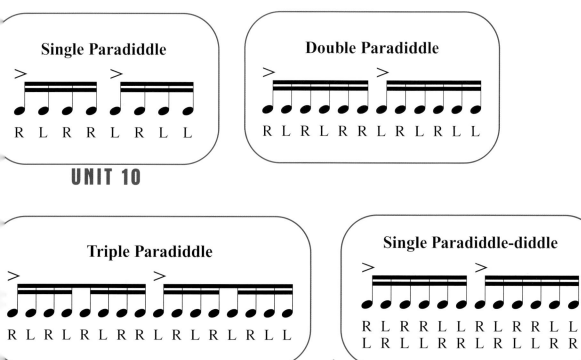

Single Paradiddle

> >

R L R R L R L L

UNIT 10

Double Paradiddle

> >

R L R L R R L R L R L L

Triple Paradiddle

> >

R L R L R L R R L R L R L R L L

Single Paradiddle-diddle

> >

R L R R L L R L R R L L
L R L L R R L R L L R R

III. FLAM RUDIMENTS

Flam

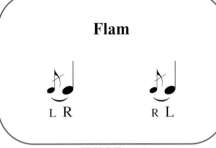

L R   R L

UNIT 12

Flam Accent

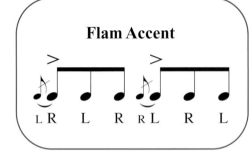

L R   L   R   R L   R   L

Flam Tap

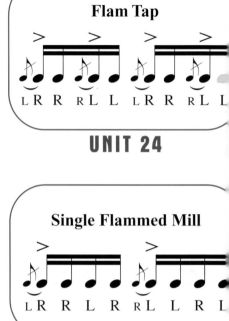

L R R   R L L   L R R   R L L

UNIT 24

Flamacue

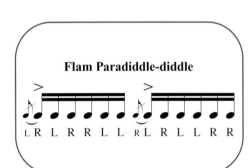

L R L R L L R
R L R L R R L

Flam Paradiddle

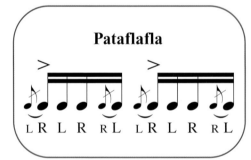

L R L R R   R L R L L

Single Flammed Mill

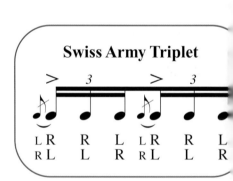

L R R L R   R L L R L

Flam Paradiddle-diddle

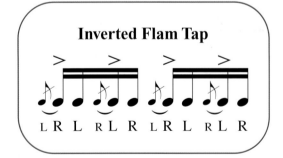

L R L R R L L   R L R L L R R

Pataflafla

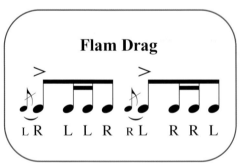

L R L R R L   L R L R R L

Swiss Army Triplet

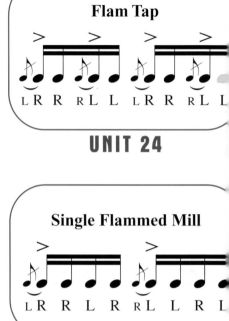

L R R L L R R L
R L R L R R L R

Inverted Flam Tap

L R L R L R   L R L R L R

Flam Drag

L R L L R R L R R L

IV. DRAG RUDIMENTS

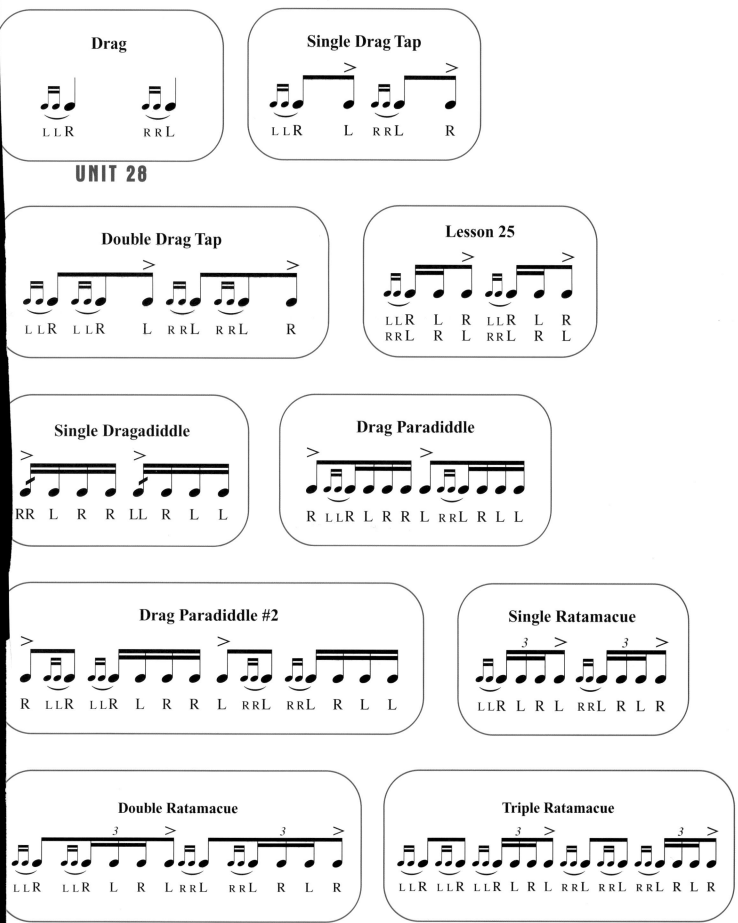

Drag

L L R   R R L

Single Drag Tap

L L R   L   r r L   R

UNIT 28

Double Drag Tap

L L R   L L R   L   R R L   R R L   R

Lesson 25

L L R   L   R   L L R   L   R
R R L   R   L   R R L   R   L

Single Dragadiddle

R R   L   R   R   L L   R   L   L

Drag Paradiddle

R   L L R   L   R   R   L   r r L   R   L   L

Drag Paradiddle #2

R   L L R   L L R   L   R   R   L   R R L   R R L   R   L   L

Single Ratamacue

3   *3*

L L R   L   R   L   R R L   R   L   R

Double Ratamacue

3   *3*

L L R   L L R   L   R   L   r r L   R R L   R   L   R

Triple Ratamacue

3   *3*

L L R   L L R   L L R   L   R   L   R R L   R R L   R R L   R   L   R

Reprinted by permission of the Percussive Arts Society, Inc., 701 NW Ferris, Lawton, OK 73507-5442:
e-mail: percarts@pas.org • web: www.pas.org

Glossary

Page numbers refer to the Student Book page where the definition is shown.

1st and 2nd Endings—*Play the 1st ending, repeat the section and play only the 2nd ending the second time.* (50)

Accent—*Play the note with more emphasis.* (50)

♯, ♭, ♮ **Accidental**—*A sharp, flat, or natural not indicated in the key signature.* (58)

Allegro—*Fast tempo.* (83)

Anacrusis—*One or more notes that come before the first full measure.* (36)

Andante—*Moderately slow (walking) tempo.* (83)

Articulation—*A slight interruption of the air stream with the tongue.* (14)

Balance—*All parts played and heard equally. The dynamic strength and importance given to instruments/voices within a composition.* (26, 66)

Bar Line—*The vertical line placed on a staff to divide the music into measures.* (14)

❜ **Breath Mark**—*A recommended place to breathe.* (14)

Canon—*Music in which the melody is introduced in one voice and echoed by another voice.* (22)

Carol—*A song of praise or celebration.* (–)

Chorale—*A slow, "hymn-like" composition.* (32)

Chord—*Three or more tones sounded at the same time.* (50)

Clef—*A symbol placed at the beginning of the staff to identify the note names on the staff.* (14)

Common Time—*4/4 time signature.* (–)

Crescendo, Cresc.—*Gradually get louder.* (124)

Da Capo, D.C.—*Return to the beginning.* (134)

D.S.—Dal Segno—*Repeat from the sign.* (151)

Decrescendo, Decresc.—*Gradually get softer.* (124)

Dot—*Increases the value of the preceding note or rest by one half.* (50)

Duet—*A piece of music with two interacting parts.* (26)

Dynamics—*Musical performance levels of loud and soft.* (36)

Embouchure—*The natural formation of the facial and lip muscles on the mouthpiece or reeds.* (14)

⌢ **Fermata**—*Hold the note or rest longer than note value.* (14, 18)

Final Bar Line—*Placed on the staff to indicate the end of a piece of music.* (14)

Fine—*The end.* (134)

♭ **Flat**—*A symbol that lowers the pitch of a note one half step.* (14)

Folk Song—*A song of cultural heritage passed from generation to generation sometimes through aural tradition.* (–)

𝆑 **Forte**—*Loud.* (36)

Grand Staff—*The Treble and Bass Clef staves joined together.* (14)

Half Step—*The distance between two adjacent notes.* (157)

Harmony—*The result of two or more tones sounded at the same time.* (26)

Improvisation—*Spontaneously creates a new melody without the intent to revise.* (151)

Interval—*The distance between two pitches.* (14, 157)

Intonation—*The accuracy of pitch or pitch relationships in the performance of music.* (18)

Introduction—*A short section of music at the beginning of a piece.* (58)

Jazz—*Music rooted in improvisation and characterized by syncopated rhythms.* (151)

Key—*The tonality of a piece of music.* (26)

Key Signature—*Flats and sharps placed immediately following the clef used to indicate which notes are to be altered throughout the piece.* (26)

Largo—*A very slow tempo.* (24)

 Ledger Lines—*Short lines placed above or below the staff for pitches beyond the range of the staff.* (14, 18)

Legato—*Smooth and connected without interruption between the notes.* (116)

March—*Music for a parade or procession.* (26)

Measure—*The space between two bar lines to form a grouping of beats.* (14)

𝄎 **Measure Repeat sign**—*A symbol that indicates to repeat the previous measure.* (106)

Melody—*A series of musical tones that form a recognizable phrase to express a composer's thoughts or statements.* (44)

𝆐𝆑 **Mezzo Forte**—*Medium loud.* (36)

Glossary *continued*

mp **Mezzo Piano**—*Medium soft.* (36)

Moderato—*Moderate or medium tempo.* (83)

Multiple Measure Rest—*A symbol indicating more than one measure of rest.* (66)

Multiple Percussion—*Playing two or more percussion instruments at the same time.* (177)

Music Alphabet—*Letter names of the notes used in music.* (14)

Musical Line—*Direction or shape of a musical thought or idea.* (26)

Natural—*A symbol which cancels a previous sharp or flat. Like a flat or sharp, it is used for the entire measure.* (58)

Ostinato—*A repeated melodic or rhythmic pattern.* (44)

Phrase—*A musical sentence or statement.* (32)

Piano—*Soft.* (36)

Rehearsal Numbers/Letters—*Markings above the staff that indicate specific locations in the music.* (66)

Repeat Sign—*Symbol that indicates to go back and play the section of music again.* (32)

‖: *Repeat from the beginning*

:‖ *Repeat of a section*

Rest—*A silent unit of time.* (18)

Rhythm—*The organization of sound and silence in time.* (14)

Ritardando, Rit.—*Gradually slowing down.* (140)

Rock—*A style of popular music which originated in America characterized by a strong rhythmic beat and electronic instruments.* (58)

Roll—*An even sustained sound on a percussion instrument.* (22)

Roll Base—*The rhythmic pattern that serves as the foundation for each roll stroke.* (22)

Rubric—*A scoring procedure that indicates different levels of achievement.* (–)

Scale—*A series of tones arranged in a set pattern from low to high or high to low forming a stepwise progression used in melodies and harmonies.* (157)

♯ **Sharp**—*A symbol that raises the pitch of a note one half step.* (14)

Sight-reading—*Reading and performing a piece of music for the first time.* (36, 66)

Slur—*A curved line placed above or below two or more different pitches to indicate that they are to be performed smoothly and connected.* (44)

Soli—*A line of music played by a small group of instruments.* (18)

Solo—*A performance by one person playing alone, with or without accompaniment.* (22)

Staccato—*Play the note lightly and detached.* (116)

Staff—*5 lines and 4 spaces on which notes and other musical symbols are placed.* (14)

Style—*The way in which music is expressed or performed.* (66)

Subdivide—*Dividing a note into smaller sections or fractions.* (36)

Swing—*A style of jazz music characterized by the "lengthening" of the eighth notes that are on the beat.* (151)

Syncopation—*Rhythm with the emphasis or stress on a weak beat or weak portion of a beat.* (140)

Tempo—*The speed of the beat.* (44)

Tenuto—*A symbol which means to play the note full value.* (116)

Tie—*A curved line connecting two notes of the same pitch and played as if they were one.* (44)

Time Signature—*A symbol placed at the beginning of the staff where the top number indicates the number of beats per measure and the bottom number what kind of note gets one beat.* (14, 106)

Tutti—*All play* (18).

Unison—*All performers sound the same note.* (26)

Whole step—*A musical distance that equals two half steps.* (157)

Stroke Dexterity Exercises

1.	R R R R	R R R R	L L L L	L L L L
2.	R R R R	L L L L	R R R R	L L L L
3.	R R R L	R R R L	R R R L	R R R L
4.	L L L R	L L L R	L L L R	L L L R
5.	R L L L	R L L L	R L L L	R L L L
6.	L R R R	L R R R	L R R R	L R R R
7.	R R L L	R R L L	R R L L	R R L L
8.	R L R L	R L R L	R L R L	R L R L
9.	R L R L	R R R R	L R L R	L L L L
10.	R L R L	R L R R	R L R L	R L R R
11.	L R L R	L R L L	L R L R	L R L L
12.	R L R L	R R L L	R L R L	R R L L
13.	L R L R	L L R R	L R L R	L L R R
14.	R L R R	L L R R	L R L L	R R L L
15.	R L R R	L R L L	R L R R	L R L L
16.	R R L R	L L R L	R L R R	L R L L
17.	R L L R	L R R L	R L L R	L R R L
18.	R L R L	R L R R	L R L R	L R L L
19.	R L R L	R R L R	L R L R	L L R L
20.	R L R L	R L L R	L R L R	L R R L